OCEANO
Langenscheidt

100 cartas-tipo
Inglés comercial

Para la correspondencia internacional

Autores:

B. Abegg
M. Benford

OCEANO

Título original:

Langenscheidts Musterbriefe. 100 Briefe Englisch

Autores:

B. Abbeg, M. Benford

© MCMXCIV Langenscheidt KG, Berlin and Munich

Para la presente edición:

© MCMXCIX OCEANO Langenscheidt Ediciones, S.L.
EDIFICIO OCEANO
Milanesat, 21-23
08017 Barcelona (España)
Teléfono: 93 280 20 20*
Fax: 93 205 25 45
http://www.oceano.com
e-mail: librerias@oceano.com

ISBN 84-95199-50-5
Impreso en España - *Printed in Spain*
Depósito legal: B-10652-99
102839495964

Prefacio

Océano Langenscheidt presenta al lector *100 cartas-tipo Inglés comercial*, un valioso manual de consulta para quien necesita escribir de forma rápida y eficaz su correspondencia comercial en inglés por correo, fax o *e-mail*.

En las pautas básicas, al principio de la obra, el usuario encontrará todo tipo de información para resolver cualquier duda sobre la redacción de la correspondencia comercial en inglés.

Siguiendo la estructura de una carta estándar, se detallan cada una de las secciones que componen un escrito comercial: membrete, referencia, fecha, etc.

Se aportan numerosos datos sobre los sistemas de reparto en Gran Bretaña y Estados Unidos, sus códigos postales respectivos, y sobre el uso del fax o del *e-mail*. También se incluye un glosario bilingüe con las abreviaturas postales más comunes.

Asimismo, el lector hallará información complementaria acerca de la partición de sílabas, el correcto uso de la puntuación, la utilización de las mayúsculas y algunas variantes de ortografía y léxico entre el inglés británico y el americano que deben tenerse en cuenta.

Los 100 modelos de carta o cartas-tipo de esta obra han sido especialmente elaborados para responder a las necesidades más comunes del sector empresarial, desde solicitudes, ofertas, pedidos, reclamaciones, correspondencia con el sector bancario o de transportes, hasta *mailings* promocionales, entre otros.

De fácil consulta y de carácter eminentemente práctico, este manual se acompaña de un glosario bilingüe, situado al margen de cada carta, con los términos más relevantes, de un índice temático ordenado alfabéticamente para facilitar la rápida localización de un término o de un tema puntual, así como de numerosas remisiones entre los modelos de carta propuestos para profundizar en determinados aspectos de contenido.

En los apéndices, han sido incluidos datos muy útiles: la moneda oficial de los países de habla inglesa, las medidas y los pesos británicos y estadounidenses, las abreviaturas comerciales más comunes, las organizaciones internacionales más relevantes y diferentes diseños de cartas y sobres.

Esta obra está avalada por la dilatada experiencia profesional de sus reconocidos autores, ambos especialistas en industria y comercio: B. Abegg y M. Benford, profesores de inglés comercial en centros especializados.

Tanto los autores como los editores de *100 cartas-tipo Inglés comercial* agradecen su colaboración y la cesión de sus cartas originales a las empresas que aparecen en esta obra.

LOS EDITORES

Índice

Características de un escrito comercial en inglés

El diseño y la estructura de una carta comercial en inglés están sujetos a usos y normas que difieren en parte de los utilizados en las cartas comerciales en español.

La fuente empleada para la realización de *100 cartas-tipo Inglés comercial* ha sido el *Guide for Typewriting*, elaborado por la British Standards Institution*.

De esta guía procede el criterio seguido para indicar las pautas sobre la distribución en la página de los elementos de una carta comercial en inglés.

Entre otros muchos temas, esta guía de referencia incluye abreviaturas, símbolos aritméticos, indicaciones acerca de la forma correcta de escribir cifras y fracciones, interlineados, etcétera.

La estructura de una carta

La carta comercial más común en inglés se compone de las secciones siguientes:

1. Membrete
2. Referencia
3. Fecha
4. Dirección del destinatario
5. Saludo
6. Asunto
7. Texto de la carta
8. Despedida
9. Firma
10. Anexo(s)
11. Posdata

Todas las secciones citadas quedan reflejadas en la carta comercial de la página siguiente a modo de ejemplo general:

---

* British Standards Institution, 2 Park Street, London W1A 2BS.

XYZ Company
PO Box 32901
London EC4T 2VC

Telephone: 0171 429 5000
Telefax: 0171 320 429

letterhead

Your ref:
Our ref: JLS/ue

reference line

3rd July 20..

date

Mr Enrique Alonso Pera
Bodegas Campos, S.A.
c/ Orense, 34
08024 Barcelona (Spain)

inside address

Dear Mr Alonso

salutation

<u>Your enquiry of 3 June 20..</u>

subject line

Thank you very much for your recent enquiry about various gin brands, which we read with great interest.

We would be glad to deliver any particular gin you require and are enclosing our latest price list and terms of delivery.

body of the letter

Please let us have your detailed enquiry. If you wish to receive any samples, we can send you a trial pack for your convenience.

We look forward to hearing from you soon.

Yours sincerely

John Smith

complimentary close

J. L. Smith
Sales Manager

name and signature

Encs

enclosures

P.S. We also enclose information about some of our special discounts.

postscript

La estructura de una carta

1. Membrete - *letterhead*

Este espacio, asignado a la identificación de la empresa remitente, incluye normalmente los siguientes elementos: nombre de la empresa, dirección, teléfono, fax y correo electrónico (*e-mail*). A veces también figuran el nombre, el cargo de la persona que lo envía y el número de despacho o la división interna correspondiente.

2. Referencia - *reference line*

Permite identificar al remitente (con sus iniciales casi siempre en mayúsculas) y a la persona que ha mecanografiado el escrito (con sus iniciales casi siempre en minúsculas). Puede figurar también la codificación del archivo correspondiente.

3. Fecha - *date*

Existen diversas posibilidades para formular esta referencia temporal:

3 February 20..	February 3rd, 20..	3 Feb 20..
February 3, 20..	February 3rd 20..	
February 3 20..	3rd February 20..	

Fecha en cifras correspondiente al 3 de febrero del 20..

03/02/20.. o 03-02-20.. (GB)
02/03/20.. o 02-03-20.. (EE UU)

4. Dirección del destinatario - *inside address*

En esta sección figuran los datos correspondientes al destinatario: el nombre, ya sea un particular o una empresa, el cargo si procede, la calle, el número, el piso y la localidad con su correspondiente código postal. A veces, se añade el nombre del departamento o la zona geográfica a la que pertenece.

Si la carta se dirige a Escocia, al País de Gales o a Irlanda del Norte, se recomienda evitar la denominación *England* (Inglaterra) y utilizar *Great Britain* (Gran Bretaña) que abarca Inglaterra, Escocia y el País de Gales o *United Kingdom* (Reino Unido) que incluye además Irlanda del Norte.

Si el destinatario es un particular o si se trata de una sociedad cuya denominación sea personalizada, suelen utilizarse las siguientes fórmulas:

Mr J. L. Smith
Mrs A. J. Gulliver
Ms Jane Mason
Miss Rosemary Thunderbell
Messrs Black & Sons

Si el destinatario es una sociedad mercantil que incluye por ejemplo: *Ltd* (GB), *plc* (GB), *Inc.* (EE UU), *Pty* (Sudáfrica), no figura: *Miss*, *Mr*, *Messrs*, etcétera:

The New York Fire Engine Inc.
Robertson & Partners Ltd
Harward & Freytag plc
Dexter & Partners Ltd

5. Saludo - *salutation*

Pese al carácter a menudo impersonal de los escritos comerciales, es preceptivo el uso de una fórmula de cortesía al comienzo de la carta. Dicha fórmula dependerá del trato que se deba dar al destinatario.

Si el destinatario es un hombre a quien ya se conoce:

Dear Mr Gulliver   Dear Adam

Si el destinatario es una mujer a quien ya se conoce:

Dear Jane   Dear Ms Mason (si se desconoce
Dear Mrs Mason (si está casada)   su estado civil)
Dear Miss Mason (si está soltera)

Si el destinatario es una empresa o alguien desconocido:

Dear Madam   Dear Sir or Madam
Dear Sir   Ladies (EE UU)
Dear Sirs   Gentlemen (EE UU)
Dear Madam, dear Sir

En cuanto a la puntuación no hay reglas fijas, pero se observa la tendencia a prescindir, por ejemplo, de los puntos en las abreviaturas y de los dos puntos o la coma tras el saludo.

Mr. / Mrs. / Ms. (EE UU)
Mr / Mrs / Ms (GB)

Dear Mr. Mason: (EE UU)
Dear Mr Mason, (GB)

6. El asunto - *subject line*

Informa del tema tratado de forma sintética. Esta línea opcional permite facilitar el archivo del documento o preparar la respuesta, y en ambos casos ahorrar tiempo. El asunto suele figurar después del saludo, sin embargo, existen algunas excepciones.

7. Texto de la carta - *body of the letter*

Respondiendo al principio de claridad, se recomienda iniciar el escrito con una breve introducción haciendo referencia al contenido de la carta que se contesta o al tema que le da origen, bien sea en un párrafo independiente o integrado en el cuerpo de la carta.

El estilo deberá ser fluido, ágil y claro.

8. Despedida - *complimentary close*

La fórmula de despedida o fórmula de cierre varía en función del lugar de destino de la carta.

En GB, el trato dado al destinatario determinará en gran medida el uso de una fórmula u otra. Cuando en el saludo se haya tratado al destinatario por su nombre, *Dear Thomas, Dr Wood, Dear Mr Smith*, se utiliza:

> Yours sincerely

Si la carta está encabezada por *Dear Sir, Dear Sirs* o *Dear Madam*, se prefiere la siguiente fórmula:

> Yours faithfully

Si se conoce bien al destinatario y el trato es informal, se utilizará una de estas fórmulas:

Sincerely	Best regards
Cordially	With best wishes
Kind regards	

En EE UU, las reglas respecto a la despedida son menos estrictas. Una carta estadounidense se concluye a menudo con:

Yours sincerely	Yours (very) truly
Sincerely yours	

9. Firma - *name and signature*

La firma da validez y crédito al contenido del escrito. Normalmente corresponde a la persona que remite la carta. A veces, una abreviatura precediendo la firma indica que se le ha otorgado ese poder a otra persona: *pp* (*per procurationem* 'por poder'). En general, la firma va acompañada del cargo del remitente.

J L Smith
Sales Manager

Helen Kessler
Personal Assistant

10. Anexo(s) - *Enc(s): enclosure(s)*

Este epígrafe, a menudo abreviado, permite desglosar toda la documentación que se adjunta, lo que ayuda a evitar extravíos, posibles malentendidos y a controlar al mismo tiempo el contenido.

11. Posdata - *P.S.: postscript*

Esta mención indica un añadido. Se trata de una nota escueta, a veces ajena al texto, relativa a un dato complementario que se ha olvidado o como recordatorio de algún detalle pendiente.

Expresiones postales más usuales

By airmail	por avión
By registered mail	por correo certificado/por correo registrado
By courier	por mensajero
Care of (c/o)	al cuidado de
For the attention of (attn)	a la atención de
Express Delivery	por expreso/entrega inmediata
If undelivered, please return	en caso de ausencia del destinatario devuélvase al remitente
To be forwarded } Please forward }	remítase al destinatario
P. O. Box	apartado de correos/casilla de correos
Poste restante } To be called for }	lista de correos
Printed matter	impresos

Printed matter reduced rate	impresos a tarifa reducida
Urgent	urgente
Confidential	confidencial
Private and confidential	privado y confidencial
Private	privado

Direcciones - Sistema de reparto británico y estadounidense - Códigos postales

En Gran Bretaña

Existen dos sistemas de reparto de correos, el *First Class Postage* y el *Second Class Postage*. Las cartas de la primera categoría se reparten más rápidamente que las de la segunda, pero su franqueo es más caro.

El código postal británico (*Postcode*) es alfanumérico, compuesto de letras y cifras. Las primeras letras indican la ciudad o la zona, y el resto la dirección del destinatario.

> PR7 SAY
> CO12 4JR

Selección de los condados de Gran Bretaña y sus abreviaturas:

Bedfordshire	Beds	North Yorkshire	N Yorks
Berkshire	Berks	Northamptonshire	Northants
Buckinghamshire	Bucks	Northumberland	Northd
Cambridgeshire	Cambs	Nottinghamshire	Notts
Gloucestershire	Glos	Oxfordshire	Oxon
Hampshire	Hants	Shropshire	Shrops/Salop
Hertfordshire	Herts	South Glamorgan	S Glam
Lancashire	Lancs	South Yorkshire	S Yorks
Leicestershire	Leics	Staffordshire	Staffs
Lincolnshire	Lincs	West Glamorgan	W Glam
Mid Glamorgan	M Glam	Wiltshire	Wilts
Middlesex	Middx	Worcestershire	Worcs

Modelo de dirección:

> Ms Anne Howard
> 2 Flora Grove
> Chorley
> Lancs
> PR7 SAY
> England

En Estados Unidos

Para realizar un envío urgente deberá figurar la mención *Priority Mail*.

El código postal estadounidense (*ZIP Code*) consta de cinco dígitos que identifican la zona de reparto. Va precedido de dos mayúsculas que remiten al estado de destino.

> MA 02116   TX 75110

Abreviaturas de los estados federales, asociados y territorios de Estados Unidos:

Alabama	AL	Kansas	KS	Ohio	OH
Alaska	AK	Kentucky	KY	Oklahoma	OK
Arizona	AZ	Louisiana	LA	Oregon	OR
Arkansas	AR	Maine	ME	Pennsylvania	PA
California	CA	Maryland	MD	Puerto Rico	PR
Canal Zone	CZ	Massachusetts	MA	Rhode Island	RI
Colorado	CO	Michigan	MI	South Carolina	SC
Connecticut	CT	Minnesota	MN	South Dakota	SD
Delaware	DE	Mississippi	MS	Tennessee	TN
District of		Missouri	MO	Texas	TX
Columbia	DC	Montana	MT	Utah	UT
Florida	FL	Nebraska	NE	Vermont	VT
Georgia	GA	Nevada	NV	Virginia	VA
Guam	GU	New Hampshire	NH	Virgin Islands	VI
Hawaii	HI	New Jersey	NJ	Washington	WA
Idaho	ID	New Mexico	NM	West Virginia	WV
Illinois	IL	New York	NY	Wisconsin	WI
Indiana	IN	North Carolina	NC	Wyoming	WY
Iowa	IA	North Dakota	ND		

Modelo de dirección:

> MS ANNE SMITH
> 782 FAIRWEATHER STREET
> BOSTON MA 02116
> USA

El fax

El fax es un sistema de comunicación rápido y eficaz que permite enviar en pocos minutos un documento a cualquier lugar del mundo. Se utiliza esta denominación tanto para referirse al soporte técnico de la transmisión como al escrito propiamente dicho. Gracias al continuo desarrollo de la tecnología, los usuarios pueden optar, hoy en día, por distintas modalidades de fax con una amplia variedad de funciones, entre las que destaca el envío programado.

Requisitos para el funcionamiento del fax

En caso de que el fax sea un módem externo, es imprescindible disponer de una línea telefónica y de papel y tinta para la recepción de los documentos. Si el fax está incorporado al módem de la computadora, es imprescindible disponer de una línea telefónica y un equipo computarizado.

Ventajas

- Rapidez: el envío se hace efectivo en escasos minutos al transmitirse la información por vía telefónica.
- Comodidad: la transmisión requiere un mínimo esfuerzo por parte del usuario.
- Eficacia: el usuario puede controlar que su mensaje haya llegado a su destino mediante un recibo que le indica una vez finalizada la transmisión que la comunicación ha sido establecida.
- Ahorro: el coste de envío es el de una simple llamada telefónica.

Inconvenientes

- Supervisión técnica: control del papel y de la tinta en caso de módem externo.
- Consumo de energía: la computadora debe permanecer encendida en caso de módem interno.
- Escasa confidencialidad: cualquier usuario puede acceder a los datos enviados.

FAX MESSAGE

From: John Smith on 0171 2804025 (Tel. and Fax)
To: Ms Ana Martínez Goma on 00 34 93 285 44 71

Date: 21 Aug 20..

Dear Ana

This is to confirm that I sent you the required documents yesterday.

Kindest regards
Yours sincerely

El *e-mail*

El correo electrónico es uno de los múltiples servicios de la red de comunicación interactiva Internet, que permite transmitir mensajes de una computadora a otra. Para ello, el remitente sólo debe indicar la dirección electrónica del destinatario y cumplimentar los datos que aparecen en pantalla. Al cliquear: "Enviar" (*Send*), el documento es transmitido al buzón (*Mailbox*) del servidor contratado, en el que permanece memorizado temporalmente. Mediante la red, llega al servidor del destinatario, y de ahí a su computadora.

Requisitos para el funcionamiento del correo electrónico

Para poder enviar o recibir mensajes es imprescindible disponer de un equipo computarizado y de una conexión a Internet a través de una línea telefónica. Existen otros tipos de conexión más rápidos aunque más costosos y complejos (sistema RDSI, conexión a una red local, etc.). Además, hace falta un programa de correo electrónico instalado y configurado, integrado en uno de los navegadores (*Browsers*) disponibles.

Ventajas

• Sencillez: no requiere conocimientos previos de computación.
• Rapidez: la transmisión es casi instantánea, excepto cuando se envían archivos adjuntos de gran tamaño (un archivo de 1MB puede tardar unos 15 minutos).
• Comodidad: el envío de los datos se realiza directamente desde la computadora, lo que favorece su clasificación y archivo.
• Ahorro económico y de tiempo: el coste de envío suele ser equivalente al de la llamada telefónica local. Además existe la posibilidad de enviar varios mensajes en una única conexión.

Inconvenientes

• Escasa confidencialidad: puede ser interceptado por algún "pirata" (*Hacker*).

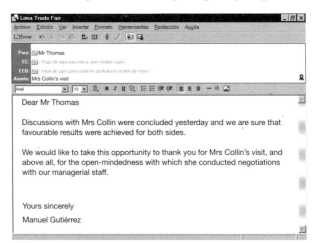

Variantes británicas y estadounidenses

Las variantes más relevantes entre la correspondencia comercial en inglés británico y americano no son tan numerosas como las utilizadas en el lenguaje coloquial o en otros ámbitos.

No obstante, cabe destacar dos aspectos fundamentales en cuanto al tema que nos ocupa: las diferencias ortográficas y de léxico.

Algunas variantes ortográficas

1. En EE UU se elimina a menudo el guión corto para separar los dos elementos que forman una palabra compuesta. Por ejemplo: *newsstand, breakdown, soapbox, cooperate*. Esta tendencia también empieza a tener aceptación en Gran Bretaña.

2. Numerosos términos, terminados en inglés británico en *-our*, acaban en inglés americano en *-or*. Por ejemplo: *color, humor, favor, honor*.

3. La terminación británica *-re* suele corresponder a la desinencia *-er* en el inglés americano. Por ejemplo: *theater, center, fiber*. Excepción: *massacre*.

4. Gran número de palabras que se terminan en inglés británico en *-gue* carecen de la desinencia *-ue*, en inglés de EE UU. Por ejemplo: *catalog, dialog*.

5. Numerosas palabras británicas que terminan en *-ce*, tienen en inglés americano la desinencia *-se*. Por ejemplo: *license, defense, practise*.

6. Mientras que en inglés británico es frecuente doblar la *-l* final de una raíz cuando la sílaba siguiente empieza en vocal, en inglés americano no suele hacerse. Por ejemplo: *dial: dialled* (GB), *dialed* (EE UU), *travel: travelled* (GB), *traveled* (EE UU).

7. La *-e-* muda desaparece en inglés americano en palabras como *abridg(e)ment, judg(e)ment* o *acknowledg(e)ment*.

8. En EE UU, además de *although, all right* y *through*, existen otros términos más informales: *altho, alright, thru*.

9. Otras diferencias de ortografía:

Inglés británico	Inglés americano
tyre	*tire*
cheque	*check*
aluminium	*aluminum*

Algunas variantes de léxico

Con el tiempo se han ido produciendo determinadas variantes entre el inglés británico y el americano. He aquí algunos ejemplos:

Inglés británico	Inglés americano
autumn	fall
underground, tube	subway
motorway	highway, freeway
queue	line
petrol (station)	gas (station)
flyover	overpass
flat	apartment, condo
ground floor	first floor
first floor	second floor
lift	elevator
pavement	sidewalk
rates	property tax
timetable	schedule
toilet	bathroom, restroom
company	corporation
public limited company	stock corporation

La partición de sílabas

A diferencia del español, las palabras inglesas no siempre pueden ser partidas en sílabas aunque valga el principio de la regla/la regla de que sólo las palabras con dos sílabas o más pueden ser separadas. Palabras como por ejemplo *asked* o *called,* son inseparables.

En general, la regla básica es que la partición permita el reconocimiento de la palabra en cuestión para facilitar su pronunciación correcta. La partición de palabras se basa, pues, en el reconocimiento de éstas. En este sentido, la palabra *listen* sólo puede ser partida entre la '*s-*' y la '*-t*': *lis-ten,* dado que una partición después de la '*t-*' incitaría al lector a pronunciar la '*t*'. Otros ejemplos similares: *co-inci-dence* (no *coin-cidence*), *coin-age* (no *co-inage*), *photo-graph* y *pho-togra-pher*.

Palabras de ortografía idéntica pero de diferente pronunciación se separan de acuerdo con este mismo criterio. Por ejemplo: *a pres-ent* y *to pre-sent* (el acento tónico varía).

Además, no se permite partir sílabas al final de una línea cuando se queden dos letras solas al principio de la siguiente, como podría ser la desinencia *-ed*. En cambio, se admiten dos letras al final de la primera línea (por ejemplo *re-produce*), aunque se recomienda evitar esta partición.

Los prefijos como *ante-* o *anti-* son inseparables.

Se pueden separar las letras dobladas, por ejemplo: *al-low, dis-solve, con-nect, as-sume, in-nocu-ous,* si esta separación no presenta los componentes de la palabra de forma equívoca (por ejemplo, *inn-keeper, call-ing, pass-ing*).

░ Sílaba tónica

18

Algunos signos de puntuación

El apóstrofo

El apóstrofo se utiliza para indicar posesión: *The Manager's car is outside. The managers' cars are outside.*

También corresponden a la forma elíptica de la tercera persona del singular del auxiliar *to be*: *The Manager's here* (*The Manager is here*).

Además, se emplea para indicar el plural de algunas cifras: *the 70's and the 80's* (en estos casos se admite también la ausencia de apóstrofo: *the 70s and the 80s*) y de palabras habitualmente invariables: *too many if's and but's.*

La coma

Es preciso poner una coma para separar una frase subordinada que no sea absolutamente necesaria para el entendimiento de la frase principal: *My brother John, who lives in London, is here.*

Las frases relativas, imprescindibles para tal comprensión, en cambio, no se separan por una coma: *The man who came yesterday is here again.*

A menudo, una coma indica una pausa, por ejemplo antes y después de *however*, *nevertheless, strangely enough*, etc.

Se puede prescindir de la coma en frases cortas con *if*. Si la frase es larga, en cambio, se pone la coma para conseguir mayor claridad de la estructura:

> *Call me if he comes.*

> *If the Managing Director asks me to contact him, I'd like you to leave a message with my secretary.*

El uso de las mayúsculas

En los escritos comerciales ingleses las mayúsculas se rigen por las mismas normas de aplicación que las de la lengua inglesa estándar.

No obstante, existen algunos casos en la correspondencia comercial en los que se admite una excepción.

Se admite el uso de la mayúscula para destacar algunas palabras. Por ejemplo *Bill of Lading, Certificate of Origin, Commercial Invoice*, etc.

Los títulos o cargos también se escriben con mayúscula. Por ejemplo: *The Manager has instructed the Finance Controller to redraft the Commercial Invoice.*

Cartas-tipo
1-100

1 Solicitud simple
Simple enquiry

25 November 20..

Clearcut Lawnmowers Ltd
90–100 Clover Drive
TORRINGTON
Kent
TZ3 8ZZ
United Kingdom

Dear Sirs

We are a newly-established firm specializing in the supply of gardening equipment. As we are currently in the process of buying in stock in good time for the coming spring season, we would be grateful if you would send us a catalogue of your full lawnmower range, both mechanical and electric.

Would you also indicate how much time should be allowed for delivery and include details of your export prices and quantity discounts. Please also state whether goods on a sale or return basis can be supplied and what your position on after-sales service is.

If your products are to good standard and delivery is prompt, we feel sure that there will be ample opportunity for your company to acquire a substantial share of the market here.

Yours faithfully
Maquinaria Gómez, S.L.

Ramón Mirallos López
Assistant Manager

newly-established recientemente establecida
gardening equipment equipos de jardinería
buy in stock comprar stocks
lawnmower segadora de césped
range gama
export price precio de exportación
quantity discounts descuentos por cantidad
sale or return compra con derecho a devolución
after-sales service servicio posventa
be to good standard ser de buena calidad
ample opportunity grandes oportunidades
share of the market parcela de mercado

February 28, 20..

Computronic Inc
PO Box 8732
Austin, TX 75110
USA

Gentlemen:

ENCRYPTION SOFTWARE

We read your advertisement in the latest edition of DataNews, in which you state that you have developed new software for the encryption of electronic data.

We are in the process of reviewing our company's security procedures and wish to introduce a hierarchical system of data access using unbreakable passwords.

We would be most interested in receiving a demonstration version of your encryption program, which we would then attempt to crack. If, using a powerful mainframe computer, we do not succeed, we will place a substantial order for your software.

We look forward to receiving your comments on this matter, together with details of on-site after-sales service and up-date facilities, should you feel that your product will pass the test we intend it to undergo.

Yours truly,
FERNÁNDEZ INFOTEC, S.L.

José Mª Martínez Robles
Software Engineer

encryption
  codificación
electronic data
  datos electrónicos
security procedure
  sistema de seguridad
data access
  acceso de datos
unbreakable passwords
  códigos infranqueables
demonstration version
  muestra de demostración
crack forzar
mainframe computer
  unidad central
comments
  observaciones
on-site in situ, sobre el terreno
after-sales service
  servicio posventa
up-date facilities
  servicio de actualización

3 Solicitud basada en una licitación
Enquiry based on a tender

TELEFAX

23 March 20..

TO: POLISH CHAMBER OF COMMERCE
FAX: +4822 274673

FROM: BILL JAMBOR, Lancashire Enterprises plc
FAX: +1773 721029

Dear Sirs

My company is at present tendering for an EU project in Romania. I would be pleased if you could send me details of Polish companies able to supply the following equipment:

1. Engine compressor spare parts, engine spare parts and pistons for "Ikarus" motor vehicles, types 260.50, 280.33, 280.64

2. Spare parts for "Tatra" Trams, type T4R

3. Electrolyte copper cathode and 18 mm diameter copper winding wire

4. Equipment and spare parts for diesel electric and electric locomotives

5. Rail coach batteries, locomotive starter batteries and locomotive storage batteries

The exact details and conditions of tender will be sent to the relevant companies.

We unfortunately have very little time to submit our tender and would thus be grateful to receive details from you as soon as possible and in any event in no later than two weeks from now.

Yours faithfully

...

tender   *aquí:* entrar en concurso
engine spare part pieza de repuesto del motor
electrolyte electrolito
copper cathode cátodo de cobre
winding wire alambres enrollados
rail coach battery batería para el vagón de ferrocarril
starter battery batería del starter
storage battery acumulador
submit presentar

Solicitud en respuesta a un anuncio
Enquiry in response to an advertisement

4

22 March 20..

A.L. Moda, S.L.
Saturnino Calleja, 48
28002 Madrid
Spain

For the attention of Marta Pérez

Dear Ms Pérez

LADIES' SUMMER WEAR

We refer to your advertisement in the this month's edition of "Fashion Plus".

We are a major importer of ladies' fashion wear with a network of retail outlets throughout the UK. For the past 10 years we have, with considerable success, been dealing in fashions for teenagers and the early 20s. Our lines are strictly up-market and are always in instant response to current trends.

Please send us your catalogue, a current export price list including terms of payment and delivery and details of quantity discounts. We would also appreciate it if you would include representative samples of some of this season's garments to enable us to assess their quality.

We feel sure that there could be considerable openings for competitively priced goods of the right design and look forward to hearing from you in good time for the coming season.

Yours sincerely
CHELSEA FASHION LTD
...

major importer importador principal
retail outlet minorista
the early 20s veinteañeros
line línea, gama
be strictly up-market *aquí:* ser de primerísima calidad
be in instant response *aquí:* responder inmediatamente
current trend tendencia actual
export price list listado de precios para la exportación
quantity discount descuentos por cantidad
openings *aquí:* oportunidades
competitively priced goods productos con precios competitivos

Lancashire Enterprises plc
Enterprise House
17 Ribblesdale Place
Winckley Square
Preston PR7 3NA

Genesis Medical Ltd
115 Gloucester Road
London S.W.7

12 December 20..

Dear Sirs

SINGLE USE TRANSFUSION SET

We were given your name by our mutual business associate, Neil Smith at Medical Systems (International) Ltd, who recommended that we contact you.

Lancashire Enterprises plc is actively involved in Eastern Europe, having won major contracts to help revitalise the industrial base of countries effecting the transition to a market economy. Included in this work is the provision of a trading service.

In this respect we have been approached by a Polish manufacturer of Single Use Transfusion Sets (sample enclosed), who has requested us to seek business contacts in Western Europe on his behalf.

As sole UK agents for the manufacturer, we are able to supply you the sets at a CIF unit price of £ .... . We are able to supply 8500 units per shipment and up to three shipments per month.

The manufacturing process used conforms to international standards. The manufacturer is in the process of applying for the Department of Health certificate and would welcome an order subject to obtaining such certification.

...../2

single use transfusion set equipo de transfusión de un solo uso
business associate socio
win major contracts conseguir contratos importantes
revitalise reactivar
effect the transition to *aquí:* en situación de transición hacia
market economy economía de mercado
provision *aquí:* facilitación
seek business contacts buscar contactos comerciales
sole agent único agente
manufacturing process proceso de fabricación
international standards normas internacionales
Department of Health Departamento de Sanidad (GB)
subject to pendiente de

In addition, if a good response from UK firms is forthcoming, the packaging will be modified and the instructions will be printed in English.

Furthermore, should you so require, the product can be modified to suit individual requirements.

We look forward to your response and would welcome an opportunity to strengthen ties with Eastern Europe. We also enclose for your information a brochure describing our activities in this field in more detail.

Yours faithfully
Lancashire Enterprises plc

Bill Jambor
Project Executive

Enc

be forthcoming
 suceder, efectuarse
suit individual
 requirements
 adecuar a
 necesidades
 individuales
strengthen ties
 with   fortalecer
 las relaciones con

June 20..

Ramírez Importación y Exportación, S.L.
Calle 13 n° 154
Bogotá 1, D.E.
COLOMBIA

Gentlemen:

Subject: Door-to-Door Delivery

Don't throw this letter away! It's worth real money to anybody who'll give us a chance to prove just how good we are!

Why worry about keeping to those delivery dates stipulated in your Sales Contract using the regular, state-owned mail service when you can make use of a custom-made personalized, door-to-door delivery service right now! We have a fleet of trucks near your town and, likely as not, based near your block, just waiting to rush your goods to their destinations.

We have already made ourselves into a household name in the US and now, by popular request, we have extended our operation to Latin America. We can provide transportation for anything from a string of pearls to a pipeline – to any destination you care to name. Just call us on a local low-toll number and we'll quote you right away. We specialize in rock-bottom priced, just-in-time delivery with full insurance cover.

We're waiting to hear from you. Just pick up that phone and call us – you'll never look back!

Sincerely yours,

...

stipulate estipular
state-owned mail service servicio público de Correos
custom-made a medida del cliente
door-to-door delivery service servicio de entrega "puerta a puerta"
fleet of trucks flota de camiones
household name nombre conocido
string of pearls collar de perlas
low-toll number llamada telefónica a precio reducido
rock-bottom price precio más bajo posible
full insurance cover seguro de cobertura total

May 21, 20..

Santamaría & Cía.
Manuel Ávila Camacho, 67
11560 México, D.F.
MÉXICO

Attn. Mr. Javier Barco Ribera

Dear Mr. Barco,

Many thanks for your enquiry of May 10 regarding the importation of our new, environmentally friendly, CFC-free packaging material.

We will have no difficulty in manufacturing and supplying the shapes you describe in the drawings included with your enquiry, since we have a molding technique which enables us to customize packaging to customers' specifications. So far, we have had an overwhelming response from all over the world to our new product and our production department is being expanded to cope with the increasing demand.

We enclose our catalog and current export price list. All prices are exclusive of tax and are quoted FCA US airport. At present, delivery to a US airport can be made within 1-2 weeks of receipt of order. We look forward to executing your order and enclose our Order Form for customer convenience.

Truly yours,
...

environmentally friendly ecológico
CFC-free no contiene CFC (productos clorofluorocarbonados)
packaging material material de embalaje
molding technique técnica de molde
customize personalizar, adaptar
catalog catálogo
exclusive of tax exento de impuestos
FCA = Free Carrier *(Incoterm)* franco transportista
Order Form hoja de pedido
for customer convenience para la conveniencia del cliente

8 Reclamación de mercancía defectuosa
Complaint about imperfect goods

7 December 20..

Turnpike Traders Ltd
Units 1–4
Greenman Industrial Estate
Blackburn
Lancashire
BB1 5QF

Dear Sirs

This morning we took delivery of the 50 boards of prime quality teak ordered as per our letter of 1 November (Order No. WW-T1-11).

The quality of 2 of the boards is, however, unsatisfactory as they contain large, unsightly knots rendering them unsuitable for use.

We feel sure that this is an oversight on your part but, owing to the considerable number of orders in hand, we had no alternative but to return the goods in question to you, carriage forward, on the assumption that you will arrange for replacements to be sent to us by return to enable us to keep to production schedules.

We trust that you will be in agreement with this course of action and look forward to receiving replacements corresponding to your otherwise high standards.

Yours faithfully
WELLING & BURBURY LIMITED

William Welling
Chief Executive

prime quality teak teca de primera calidad
unsatisfactory deficiente, insatisfactorio
unsightly feo, antiestético
unsuitable for use inadecuado para su uso
oversight descuido
order in hand pedidos realizados
carriage forward a portes debidos
by return a vuelta de correo
keep to cumplir con
production schedule planificación (de producción)
be in agreement with estar de acuerdo con
high standard alto nivel de calidad

March 26, 20..

Lorenzo Infotec
Av. Corrientes, 302
1043 Buenos Aires
ARGENTINA

Attn: Mr. Antonio Serrano Torres

Dear Mr. Serrano:

Subject: Complaint re DRT/398 Semi-conductors

Thank you for your communication of March 10, in which you state that the semi-conductors supplied are not up to standard.

Having looked into the matter we are now able to tell you that you were mistakenly supplied with DRT/298 semi-conductors, which, despite having similar properties to the latest version, are not able to perform as consistently as their successor.

We apologize for the inconvenience caused and would suggest that we either take back the consignment, carriage forward with insurance covered by us and replace it by DRT/398s, or reduce the price of the goods you have received to the standard list-price, with a further discount of 10% to make up for the inconvenience caused.

Please fax us your reply at your earliest convenience. Should you opt for a replacement delivery we will rush the goods to you by airmail.

Sincerely yours,
...

re   respecto a
be up to standard
  ser del nivel de
  calidad requerido
look into the matter
  investigar el asunto
**be mistakenly
  supplied**
  ser suministrado
  por error
similar property
  propiedad similar
inconvenience
  molestia
consignment
  remesa
**with insurance
  covered by us**
  con el seguro
  a nuestro cargo
make up for
  compensar
opt for   optar por
**replacement
  delivery**   envío
  de reposición

10 Solicitud de un informe bancario
Application for a bank reference

15 February 20..

Benson Bank plc
42 Leadenhall Street
London EC1 7HJ

Dear Sir or Madam

A. P. Jones & Sons Limited
Account Number 28625309

The above-mentioned customer has approached us requesting a credit facility amounting to £15,000 per month on 30-day terms.

We would be most grateful if you would advise us whether the company in question is sufficiently sound for such a facility.

Should you so prefer, please feel free to reply via our bankers, SouthWest plc, Hounslow Bath Road Branch, Middlesex MX1 4WW quoting our account number 29560277.

Any information given will, of course, be treated in the strictest confidence with no obligation on your part.

Yours faithfully
INTERFORM LTD

P. J. Smith
Managing Director

approach s.o.
dirigirse a alg.
credit facility
crédito
on 30-day terms
condiciones de
pago a 30 días
advise *aquí:*
comunicar
sound sólida
via a través de
our bankers
nuestro banco
account number
número de cuenta
in the strictest
confidence
en la más estricta
confidencialidad
with no obligation
on your part sin
ningún compromiso
por su parte

Informe bancario desfavorable
Unfavourable bank reference

28 February 20..

Charles Cape & Co Ltd
42 New Fetter Lane
London EC1A 4WW

Dear Sirs

Easifit Car Accessories Limited

In response to your request for a reference regarding the above-mentioned firm, we must point out that the firm in question has not been known to us for long.

We are thus unable to furnish you with the information you require.

We regret not being in a position to assist you in this matter.

Yours faithfully
NorthEast Bank plc

T. B. Smith
Assistant Manager
Corporate Accounts Dept.

accessory
  accesorio
in response to
  en respuesta a
point out
  señalar
firm in question
  empresa en
  cuestión
**furnish s.o. with
  s. th.** proveer
  a alg. de algo
be in a position
  estar en
  condiciones de
**Corporate
  Accounts Dept.**
  Departamento
  Corporativo
  de Cuentas

12 Informe bancario sin compromiso
Non-committal bank reference

March 31, 20..

Juan López & Cía.
6 Avenida, 26 Zona 10
Ciudad de Guatemala
GUATEMALA

STRICTLY CONFIDENTIAL

Gentlemen:

Thank you for enquiry regarding the company you refer to in your letter of March 15.

Due to the fact that we have only held the subject's account for some six months now we are not able to assist you in this matter.

We regret not being able to help you this time.

Sincerely yours,

Thomas G. Slade
Business Accounts Division

due to the fact that dado el hecho de que
hold an account llevar una cuenta
subject *aquí:* cliente, empresa
assist ayudar, atender
Business Accounts Division División de Cuentas Comerciales

Solicitud de referencias de crédito
Request for a credit reference

➡ carta 14

Giménez Import-Export, S.L.
Avenida de los Héroes, 24
San Salvador
EL SALVADOR

U2/45
23 July 20..

Hamlyn Engineering
Golden Crescent
Hayes
Middlesex MX1 UB3
England

PRIVATE AND CONFIDENTIAL

Dear Sirs

We have recently been approached by the firm mentioned on the enclosed slip, who have requested us to grant them a credit facility amounting to £5,000 per quarter. We understand from the firm in question that you have been dealing with them for some time and they have suggested that we request you to supply an appropriate trade reference.

We would be grateful if you would kindly reply to the following questions to enable us to conclude whether the business of subject is sufficiently sound to support the facility mentioned. Your early response using the stamped addressed envelope enclosed would be much appreciated.

1. How long has subject been known to you?
2. What amount of credit facility do you normally allow subject?
3. On what terms do you trade with subject?

.../2

private and confidential privado y confidencial
grant conceder
slip hoja, ficha
credit facility crédito
per quarter por trimestre
appropriate apropiado
trade reference informe comercial
business of subject *aquí:* la empresa en cuestión
sound sólido
support respaldar
addressed envelope sobre con dirección
subject *aquí:* la empresa en cuestión

4. Are payments made promptly/slowly/very slowly?
5. Have you ever had occasion to threaten to take legal proceedings to recover sums due to you?
6. Please also give any other information you feel is relevant.

We assure you that any information given will be treated in the strictest confidence. Please do not hesitate to contact us in future should you require us to reciprocate.

Yours faithfully
Giménez Import-Export, S.L.

Jesús Camacho
Managing Director

Enc

take legal proceedings
emprender procedimientos judiciales
recover sums
recuperar cantidades
due to s. o.
debido a alg.
treat tratar
reciprocate *aquí:* devolver un favor

Informe favorable de referencias de crédito
Favourable credit reference from a firm

14

➡ carta 13

30 July 20..

Giménez Import-Export, S.L.
Avenida de los Héroes, 24
San Salvador
EL SALVADOR

CONFIDENTIAL

Dear Mr. Camacho

In response to your letter dated 23 July 20..,
ref. No. U2/45, we are pleased to supply you with
the following information.

The firm in question are well established on the
local market and have a good reputation. As far as
we know they have been trading for over 15 years
in our field of enterprise and have built up a sizeable network of overseas customers.

We have been dealing with them for the past
8 years now on quarterly account terms and are
pleased to report that they have always met their
financial commitments punctually and in full.
We have, thus far, extended them a credit line of
up to £2,500 in any given quarter but would have
no hesitation in increasing it to double this figure,
should the need arise.

We trust that this information will be of use to
you and would point out that it is given in the
strictest confidence with no obligation whatsoever
on our part.

Yours sincerely
HAMLYN ENGINEERING

Harry Hamlyn
Chief Executive

field of enterprise
  ámbito de empresa
build up   crear
sizeable
  considerable,
  importante
network   red
overseas
  desde GB: exterior
  si no: transatlántico
on quarterly
  account terms
  en condiciones
  trimestrales
meet one's financial
  commitments
  cumplir uno con
  sus compromisos
  financieros
extend   *aquí:*
  conceder
credit line   línea
  de crédito
in any given
  quarter   en
  cualquier trimestre
on our part
  por nuestra parte

37

28 April 20..

Coupre Links 401
9000 GENT
Belgium

Fax: + 32 56 773058

Dear Sir or Madam

RE: SOURCING GINSENG ROOTS

With reference to our fax of 22 April please note that our contacts in China have just confirmed that small samples and descriptive literature have been despatched. As soon as we receive this material we will pass it on to you.

The price CIF Antwerp is generally something in the region of US$ 25 per kg - types, quality, minimum order quantity, delivery etc to be confirmed.

In the meantime we would appreciate some information on your company's background and financial standing. We would point out at this juncture that it is to be expected that the Chinese supplier will stipulate payment by letter of credit.

Should you have any queries please do not hesitate to contact us.

Yours faithfully
Lancashire Enterprises plc

Mannix Fu
Project Executive / Trade Dept.

source encontrar
una fuente
de suministro
root raíz
sample muestra
descriptive
literature folletos
informativos
despatch enviar
be something in the
region of
alrededor de,
del orden de
minimum order
quantity cantidad
mínima por pedido
financial standing
situación financiera
at this juncture
en este momento
stipulate estipular
payment by letter
of credit pago a
través de una carta
de crédito
Trade Dept.
Departamento
Comercial

18 February 20..

Prince DIY Centre
75 – 95 New Hall Street
Oxford OX1 7HH

Dear Customer

DIY ON YOUR DOORSTEP!

We are delighted to report that customer demand for our unbeaten range of "do-it-yourself" equipment and materials has increased at such a staggering pace, that we are shortly to be opening a second branch just outside town on the new Pricewise Trading Estate.

Our new branch, at 42 – 50 Grove Road, will provide ample parking facilities and will stock all the lines you have come to know and rely on together with a whole new range of modestly priced accessories for the DIY-enthusiast working on his own. This range will include "one-hand" tools enabling the handiman (or woman!) to manipulate equipment with one hand only, leaving the other free.

Just to convince you how serious we are, we're offering a 5% discount on all cash sales over £25 during the first month of business as from the first of next month. We'll deliver all bulky items (marked with a red star on the price tag) to your front door absolutely free of charge within a 25-mile radius.

So don't miss the chance of cashing in on our once-in-a-lifetime throw-away offers! We're looking forward to greeting you on our new premises on June 1st and we're absolutely certain you'll be glad you came!

Yours faithfully
...

DIY = do-it-yourself hágalo Ud. mismo
at a staggering pace a un ritmo asombroso
parking facilities servicio de aparcamiento
modestly priced accessories accesorios a un precio módico
"one-hand" tool herramienta para utilizar con una sola mano
handiman *aquí:* aficionado al bricolage
cash sale pago en efectivo
bulky voluminoso
price tag etiqueta
within a 25-mile radius en un radio de 25 millas
miss the chance perder la oportunidad
once-in-a-lifetime una vez en la vida
a throw-away offer oferta única

17 Emisión de un crédito documentario irrevocable
Issue of an irrevocable documentary credit

12 September 20..

Torrington Marine Co Ltd
Unit 8
Greenway Industrial Estate
Blackburn
BA3 8IJ
Lancashire

Dear Sirs

We have been requested by the Bank of International Commerce in the Sultanate of Oman to advise the issue of their irrevocable Credit Number 344912/02 in your favour for account of

MidEast Marine

of Kuwi, Sultanate of Oman, P.O. Box 61842, for £25,000 (SAY TWENTY-FIVE THOUSAND POUNDS STERLING) available by your drafts on us at 30 days sight accompanied by the following documents:

1. Signed invoices in triplicate certifying goods are in accordance with order No. 2092/02 dated 15 August 20.. between MidEast Marine and Torrington Marine Co Ltd.

2. Marine and War Risk Insurance Certificate covering "All risks" warehouse to warehouse, for 10% above the CIF value, evidencing that claims are payable in the Sultanate of Oman.

3. Complete set 3/3 Shipping Company's clean "on board" ocean Bills of Lading made out to order of the shippers and endorsed to order of the Bank of International Commerce, Sultanate of Oman,

...../2

for account of
   por cuenta de
draft on us
   giro a nuestro
   nombre
at 30 days sight
   a 30 días vista
invoice   factura
in triplicate
   por triplicado
**marine and war
   risk insurance
   certificate**
   certificado de
   seguro de envío
   marítimo y contra
   riesgo de guerra
all risks   a todo
   riesgo
**clean "on board"
   ocean bill of
   lading**
   conocimiento de
   embarque marítimo
   a bordo limpio
make out to order
   emitir a la orden de
endorse   endosar

marked "Freight Paid" and "Notify MidEast Marine of Kuwi, Sultanate of Oman, P.O. Box 61842".

Covering: 3x Type 500-D Outboard Motors CIF Muscat
Shipped from UK Port to Muscat
Partshipment prohibited
Transhipment prohibited
Documents must be presented for payment within 15 days from the date of shipment.

We are requested to add our confirmation to this Credit and we hereby undertake to pay you the face amount of your drafts drawn within its terms, provided such drafts bear the number and date of the Credit and that the Letter of Credit and all amendments thereto are attached.

The Credit is subject to Uniform Customs and Practices for Documentary Credits (1994 Revision), International Chamber of Commerce Publication No. 500.

Drafts shown under this Credit must be presented to us for payment/negotiation/acceptance not later than 12 October 20.. and marked "Drawn under Credit Number 344912/02" of the Bank of International Commerce Sultanate of Oman.

Dated ...

Signed ...

pp
York Bank plc
91 Mosley Street
Manchester MA1 3UZ

freight paid flete pagado
outboard motor fueraborda
partshipment embarques parciales
transhipment transbordo
undertake comprometerse a
face amount valor nominal
amendment modificación, corrección
attach adjuntar
be subject to estar sujeto a
uniform uniforme, estandarizado
negotiation negociación, tramitación
acceptance aceptación

18 Orden de un pedido específico
Placing a specific order

➡ cartas 19–22

17 October 20..

Lupton Bros Ltd
P.O. Box 8
Fountain Works
Portland Street
Accrington
Lancashire
BB5 1RJ
England

Dear Sirs

OUR PURCHASE ORDER NO. 5769F/KED

We refer to your fax No. 0254 36279 dated
5 October 20.. relating to our enquiry No. 921/KED
and wish to place an order for the following items:

QTY.	DESCRIPTION	U. PRICE	T. PRICE
5,000	Rubberized spindles for Northrop looms	£0.80	£4,000.00
	Khedival mail line (agency)		£40.00
	Legalization and certification		£150.00
	TOTAL PRICE FOB		£4,190.00

(SAY FOUR THOUSAND ONE HUNDRED AND
NINETY POUNDS STERLING ONLY)

.../2

purchase order
   pedido
place an order
   hacer un pedido
item   artículo
qty = quantity
   cantidad
description
   descripción
u. price = unit price
   precio unitario
t. price = total price
   precio total
rubberized spindle
   huso para hilar
   resinado
loom   telar
legalization
   legalización
certification
   certificación

TERMS

PRICES The above prices are firm and subject to no future change and are quoted FOB, packing included.

N.B. Kindly let us have a new Proforma Invoice in 10 (ten) copies, showing FOB prices, fixed delivery period and terms of payment.

PAYMENT Against a confirmed L/C only. Should any extension of the validity of the credit be necessary as a result of your being at fault, extra expenses incurred will be charged to you.

N.B. This order is subject to the approval of the appropriate Egyptian authorities and to the opening of the necessary credit in your favour.

DELIVERY 4 months from opening of L/C.

INSURANCE & FREIGHT As per our circulars enclosed.

CONDITIONS OF SHIPMENT Shipment by container is not allowed.
Shipment to be effected through:

KHEDIVAL MAIL LINE (AGENCY)
AIRWORK HOUSE
35 PICCADILLY
L O N D O N

We look forward to receiving your confirmation and remain

Yours faithfully
SOCIÉTÉ MISR DE FILATURE
ET DE TISSAGE FIN

firm fijo, invariable
be subject to estar sujeto a
packing included embalaje incluido
pro-forma invoice factura proforma
fixed delivery period plazo de entrega establecido
terms of payment condiciones de pago
confirmed L/C carta de crédito confirmada
extension prórroga, extensión
validity validez
be at fault aquí: de su demora, también: por su causa
extra expenses gastos extra
incur suceder, ocurrir
shipment embarque
confirmation confirmación

19 Confirmación de pedido
Confirmation of Order

→ cartas 18,
20 – 22

1 November 20..

Your ref.: 5769F/KED
Our ref.: GE/tt

Société Misr de Filature
et de Tissage Fin
KAFR EL DAWAR A.R.E.
EGYPT

Dear Sirs

Thank you for your letter of 17 October.

We hereby confirm your Purchase Order No. 5769
F/KED for 5,000 rubberized spindles for Northrop
looms, total price £4,190.00, FOB UK port,
payment to be made by confirmed L/C.

We note your Conditions of Shipment and confirm
that the order will be effected as per the provisions
of your Insurance and Freight Circulars.

As requested we enclose a new pro forma invoice
and ten copies thereof.

We trust the goods will arrive punctually and in
good condition and look forward to doing further
business with you in the future.

Yours faithfully
LUPTON BROS LTD

G. Etherington
Export Manager

Encs

rubberized spindle
huso para hilar
resinado
loom   telar
confirmed L/C
carta de crédito
confirmada
note   tomar nota
effect   llevar a cabo
as per   de acuerdo
con, según
provision
disposición
**Insurance and
Freight Circular**
circular acerca
de seguro y flete
trust   confiar

44

Société Misr de Filature
et de Tissage Fin
KAFR EL DAWAR A.R.E.
EGYPT

➡ cartas 18, 19, 21, 22

INSURANCE AND FREIGHT CIRCULAR

Dear Sirs

Further to our attached order we wish to draw your attention to our Insurance & Shipping Instructions and would point out that they are also those observed by ourselves.

1. SHIPPING METHOD
(a) Goods must be transported in the hold of the ship.
(b) Shipping to be effected using ships not more than 20 years old and also according to the Institute of London Underwriters classification clause.

2. SHIPPING INSTRUCTIONS
All cases should be marked S.M. followed by the number of the case, followed by the total number of cases in the consignment.

Example: If the cases are part of order 8706 and the total number of cases in the consignment amounts to 4, the cases should be marked:

S.M./8706/1/4   S.M./8706/2/4   S.M./8706/3/4
S.M./8706/4/4

When despatching the order please airmail us the NAME of the SHIP on which the goods are to be shipped and the number of the purchase order relating to the consignment. This information will be of great assistance to us in tracing the goods upon their arrival at port and in proceeding with their clearance through customs immediately, thus avoiding delay.

.../2

attached adjunto
shipping method condiciones de embarque
hold bodega
effect shipping embarcar
according to de acuerdo con
underwriter compañía aseguradora
classification clause cláusula de clasificación
consignment envío, remesa
despatch enviar, despachar
purchase order orden de compra
be of assistance ser de ayuda
trace *aquí:* localizar
proceed with *aquí:* proceder con
clearance through customs despacho de aduanas

3. DETAILS TO BE COMMUNICATED TO US

Please arrange for us to receive, at least 24 hours before sailing date, details of the consignment together with the following information to enable us to effect the required insurance:
(a) Name of the carrying ship
(b) Value of the goods despatched
(c) Port of loading

Before shipping any consignment, the value of which amounts to or exceeds E£30,000 (thirty thousand Egyptian pounds) at any one time, the above information must be communicated to us.

TELEGRAPHICALLY

For ordinary orders the information, as specified above, can be sent by AIRMAIL letter.
N.B.   Failure to communicate details to us telegraphically, as specified above, will oblige us to hold you responsible for any decision prejudicial to ourselves in connection with our open insurance policy.

4. FREIGHT

"From port of despatch to Alexandria port", to be payable at destination, in "EGYPTIAN CURRENCY".

5. CLEARANCE

To enable us to clear the goods through customs please airmail us the appropriate invoice, packing and specification lists in 10 (ten) copies or more if possible.

In this respect we would draw your attention to the fact that by sending your invoices and packing lists etc as requested you will save us a considerable amount of time and will, above all, avoid complications with our customs authorities.

Please follow the above instructions for all consignments sent against our orders. We depend on your co-operation for us to receive the information required in good time.

Yours faithfully
...

---

sailing date
  fecha de salida (de barcos)
port of loading
  puerto de embarque
amount to
  ascender a
exceed   exceder
failure   *aquí:*
  la omisión
oblige s.o.
  obligar a alg.
hold s.o. responsible
  responsabilizar a alg.
prejudicial
  perjudicial
open insurance policy   póliza
  (de seguros) abierta
port of despatch
  puerto de embarque
destination
  destino
currency   moneda
clearance   *aquí:*
  despacho (de aduanas)
invoice   factura
packing list   lista de contenido,
  packing list
customs authorities
  autoridades aduaneras
depend on
  depender de
co-operation
  colaboración
in good time
  a tiempo

Notificación de envío
Advice of Despatch

21

➡ cartas 18–20, 22

Lupton Bros Ltd
P.O. Box 8
Accrington
Lancashire BB5 1RJ
England

1 January 20..

Your ref.: 5769F/KED
Our ref.: GE/tt

Société Misr de Filature
et de Tissage Fin
KAFR EL DAWAR A.R.E.
EGYPT

Dear Sirs

Your Purchase Order No. 5769F/KED

We are pleased to inform you that the goods ordered as per the above mentioned purchase order have been despatched in accordance with your instructions.

They have been packed in 5 cases, 100 to a case. The cases are marked S.M./5769F/KED and numbered 1-5/5.

The consignment is being shipped on board MV "Egyptian Star", which is due to leave Southampton at the end of this month, arriving in Alexandria on 15 March.

We have handed our sight draft for £4,190.00 to the Arabian Bank, London together with the documents required under the terms of the L/C, namely: a complete set of clean, shipped on board Bs/L

.../2

purchase order
  orden de compra
in accordance with
  de acuerdo con
100 to a case
  100 por caja
on board (a vessel)
  a bordo
  (de un buque)
MV= motor vessel
  buque, barco de
  motor
sight draft
  letra a la vista
L/C = letter of
  credit carta
  de crédito
complete set
  juego completo,
  remesa completa
clean B/L
  conocimiento de
  embarque limpio

endorsed to your order, marked in accordance with your specifications; one original and ten copies of the commercial invoice; a certificate of UK origin duly legalized by the Arab Republic of Egypt Representation; a declaration from the Egyptian Company for Maritime Transport "Martrans", evidencing that the goods have been shipped by them; a packing list; insurance certificate in triplicate.

The Arabian Bank has paid the sum.

We trust that the goods will be to your complete satisfaction and look forward to hearing from you again. We also enclose for your information some changes to our current price-list.

Yours faithfully
LUPTON BROS LTD

G. Etherington
Export Manager

Enc

endorse endosar
commercial invoice
  factura comercial
certificate of origin
  certificado
  de origen
duly legalized
  debidamente
  legalizado
maritime transport
  transporte marítimo
evidence
  probar
packing list
  lista de contenidos,
  packing list
insurance certificate
  póliza de seguro
in triplicate
  por triplicado
be to one's
  complete
  satisfaction
  ser de plena
  satisfacción
  para alg.

Reclamación
Complaint

➡ cartas 18–21

20 March 20..

Lupton Bros Ltd
P.O. Box 8
Accrington
Lancashire BB5 1RJ
ENGLAND

Dear Sirs

Our Purchase Order No. 5769F/KED

With reference to the above-mentioned order for 5,000 rubberized spindles we regret to advise you that checks have revealed that the rubber at the base of approx. 40% of the spindles is in an unsatisfactory condition. It would appear that the rubber is perished owing to storage in strong sunlight or as a result of having been left outside for a prolonged period of time. We have airmailed you a sample spindle under separate cover for you to inspect yourselves.

You will appreciate that we are unable to install the defective parts in our looms and are therefore forced to run our mill at reduced capacity. This, in turn, has caused delays in delivery for our clients, who, should the delay continue, will have no alternative but to seek an alternative source of supply.

We therefore need 2,000 replacements in perfect condition immediately and would suggest that you despatch them to us by air freight, carriage paid.

We feel obliged to point out that your handling of this matter will determine whether we will be able to continue our business relationship in future.

Yours faithfully
SOCIÉTÉ MISR DE FILATURE
ET DE TISSAGE FIN
...

rubberized spindle huso resinado para hilar
reveal revelar, desvelar
to be perished estar deteriorado, dañado
storage almacenaje
in strong sunlight a plena luz del sol
prolonged prolongado, largo
appreciate *aquí:* darse cuenta de, percibir
install instalar
loom telar
mill fábrica
source of supply fuente de suministro
replacement repuesto
by air freight carga aérea
carriage paid transporte pagado
handling manejo

10 May 20..

MacGraw Landfill Inc.
PO box 25376
St. Louis, MO 63178
USA

Gentlemen:

As per your Order No. 231/ZH of April 30 we have despatched a VX 78 tire shredder to you using InterTrans as freight forwarders. They, in turn, advise us that the machine will be shipped on board MV "Ariadne" which is due to leave Santander on May 15 and will dock in Norfolk, Virginia at the end of June.

Under the FCA terms agreed the machine will be placed at your disposal at InterTrans' depot in St. Louis by June 30 at the latest.

Sincerely yours,
MUÑOZ DÍAZ, S.L.

Javier Moreno
Export Manager

tire shredder neumáticos desmenuzados
freight forwarder agente de transportes
in turn a su vez, por su parte
MV = motor vessel buque, barco de motor
be due to leave tener previsto salir
dock atracar (muelle)
depot almacén

Aceros Blanco, S.L.
Cerrito 537 casilla 1445
11.000 Montevideo
REPÚBLICA DEL URUGUAY

2nd May 20..

Dear Mr Salvador

Our Order 19345692 TI

Thank you for your telex of April 25 in which you state that the steel plates will be ready for dispatch and awaiting shipment in a fortnight's time.

In our L/C we stipulate that we require a commercial invoice, the B/L and the insurance certificate for shipment CIF Bangkok together with a quality control report. As regards this latter we have entrusted the company we name below with quality control and they will be contacting you in the next few days. They are:

SGS
Société Générale de Surveillance
Uruguayan Office Montevideo

Would you please enclose this company's assessment with the documentation to be presented to both the issuing and the advising banks.

Thank you in advance for your help.

Yours sincerely
SOUTH EAST ASIA STEEL
...

steel plate
placa de acero
await shipment
esperar para
embarcar
L/C = letter of credit   carta
de crédito
commercial invoice
factura comercial
B/L = bill of lading
conocimiento de
embarque
insurance certificate
póliza de seguros
quality control report   informe
de control de
calidad
entrust   encomendar
assessment
aquí: evaluación,
valoración
issuing bank
banco emisor
(carta de crédito)
advising bank
banco ordenante
(carta de crédito)

10 April 20..

Peterson & Jones Pty
P.O. Box 395
Cape Town
SOUTHAFRICA

Dear Mr Wilde

Our Enquiry PL/384 of 2nd March 20..
Your Offer No. 58391 of 21st March 20..

We are pleased to inform you that your DX 33 saw-blades wholly conform to our quality requirements. We should therefore like to place an order for 25 units, provided you can see your way clear to granting us a further rebate of 5% on your prices as quoted in the above-mentioned offer. We feel that the volume of the order we are interested in placing would justify this small concession.

However, to enable us to import these saw-blades into India we will need to apply for an import licence from our local Government authorities and would therefore ask you to send us a pro-forma invoice to include the following details:

- exact description of the goods
- unit and total price with discounts
- terms of payments and delivery CIF Calcutta
- packing list

We would be grateful if you would send the pro-forma invoice by registered mail. As soon as we have received the import licence, we shall telex our order to you and open the L/C with our bankers.

Yours sincerely

...

saw-blade hoja de sierra
conform to ajustarse a
unit unidad
grant otorgar, conceder
rebate reducción, baja
volume of the order volumen de pedido
justify justificar
import licence licencia de importación
authority autoridad
pro-forma invoice factura proforma
packing list lista de contenidos, *packing list*
by registered mail por correo certificado
open the L/C abrir la carta de crédito

Envío de la factura
Sending the invoice

Your ref: HJ/ly
Our ref: MPM/fa

7 January 20..

Mr Arthur M Jones
Laser Engineering Ltd
1 Victoria Square
Birmingham B1 1BD
UNITED KINGDOM

Dear Mr Jones

Your Order 835/XI of 15 Dec 20..

We are pleased to inform you that the articles, as per the above-mentioned order, were despatched by lorry yesterday. They will be shipped across the Channel on board SS Marina tomorrow and are due to arrive at your premises at the beginning of next week.

Please find enclosed our invoice No. 351 685 T for Euros 36,000.00 including all transport costs. We would ask you to settle it either by bank transfer or by cheque within 30 days, subject to the usual early payment discount of 3 per cent.

We trust that you will receive the goods in perfect condition and remain at your service for further deliveries at any time.

Yours sincerely
Hernández García, S.L.

María Peralta Molina
Export Dept.

by lorry
  por camión
the Channel
  El Canal de
  la Mancha
premises   local,
  oficina(s)
transport costs
  costes de transporte
settle   *aquí:*
  liquidar
by bank transfer
  por transferencia
  bancaria
by cheque
  por cheque
the usual early
  payment discount
  el descuento
  habitual por
  pronto pago
further deliveries
  envíos futuros

27 Solicitud de cuenta abierta
Request for open account terms

November 25, 20..

Seaboard Industries plc
Grand Avenue
Hove
East Sussex BN3 2LS
Great Britain

Gentlemen:

As you know, we have been customers of your company for almost two years now and have always settled our invoices punctually by letter of credit in the pre-agreed way.

This is why we feel that we can now request you to grant us payment on open account terms for further deliveries, viz a 3-month payment period against presentation of your quarterly statement.

We feel that we have now earned this short-term credit facility, particularly because we aim to be placing further and possibly more substantial orders with you in the near future.

Awaiting your news with interest,

Yours very truly,
Marting & Campals Inc.

Christopher P. Jefferson
Assistant Manager

settle an invoice liquidar una factura
letter of credit carta de crédito
in the pre-agreed way en la forma preestablecida
viz = videlicet, namely verbigracia, es decir
a 3-month payment period un período de pago de 3 meses
presentation presentación
quarterly statement extracto trimestral
short-term credit facility facilidades del crédito a corto plazo
more substantial orders pedidos más considerables

12 July 20..

Ms Maria de Lurdes Fontes Pereira
Fontes & Melo Ltda.
Rua de D. Afonso Henriques, 49
P-1300 Lisboa
PORTUGAL

Dear Ms Pereira

<u>Balancing of Our Quarterly Account
to June 30th 20..</u>

We confirm the receipt of your quarterly account showing a debit balance for us of £475.50.

After comparing your statement with our figures, however, we find that there is a discrepancy. According to our records our debit balance only amounts to £375.50. We have checked our invoices thoroughly and have been unable to find any irregularities in our payments. Could it be that your figure is a misprint?

We have of today advised our Invoicing Department to remit the equivalent of £375.50 in Euros to your account by bank transfer and would request you to check your figures once again. Should you arrive at a figure differing from ours, please let us know, specifying the exact nature of the difference of £100.00, for which we ourselves have no explanation.

We hope that this matter can be solved quickly and without any further inconvenience. For your information we are sending you enclosed a copy of our own statement.

Yours sincerely

...

quarterly trimestral
debit balance saldo deudor
statement extracto
discrepancy discrepancia
record registro
thoroughly minuciosamente
irregularity irregularidad
Invoicing Department Departamento de Facturación
remit remitir, enviar
equivalent equivalente
arrive at a figure obtener un resultado
differ diferir

The Clock Company Ltd
Addison Avenue
St. Albans
Herts SA3 1AD

25 September 20..

Patel Trading Co Ltd
Units 4-8 Industrial Estate
Blackburn
Lancs NL3 4 WW

Dear Mr Patel

"Pocket Travelite" Alarm Clock

Our representative in the north of England informs us that you are in the market for electronic travelling alarm clocks. We are pleased to tell you that our latest model, the "Pocket Travelite", has just been launched and will most certainly suit your customers' requirements as regards price, quality, size and performance.

Our company has now been operating in this field for more than five years and in this time we have conducted in-depth market research into customer expectations. Our new "Pocket Travelite" has been tailor-made to correspond to the findings of our customer surveys and we have every confidence in its success. The new model's specifications are as follows:

Casing:	durable and shock-resistant matt plastic case in black, white or burgundy
Battery:	1.5 V, lasts one year on average
Size:	5 cm x 5 cm x 3 cm
Weight:	150 g

.../2

representative
representante
be in the market
for querer vender
launch lanzar
performance
rendimiento
operate operar
conduct dirigir,
conducir
in-depth
en profundidad
market research
investigación de
mercado
tailor-made
hecho a medida
finding
conclusiones
survey encuesta,
sondeo
confidence
confianza
durable duradero
shock-resistant
a prueba de golpes

Features: illuminable digital display; snooze/re-
           peat function; alarm tone increases in
           volume
Guarantee: 12 months

Servicing: Free, except in cases of misuse,
           throughout guarantee period
Price: £12.00 per unit

Should you opt to place an initial order for over
100 units we will be pleased to grant you a
discount of 10% on the price quoted.

We enclose a sample clock for your inspection
together with the full sales literature. Our conditions of sale and delivery are as is customary in
the trade and are set out in detail in our brochure.

We look forward to your comments on our offer.

Yours sincerely
THE CLOCK COMPANY Ltd

A.P.T. Smith
Sales Manager

Encs

digital display
  pantalla digital
servicing
  mantenimiento
  y reparación
misuse   mal uso,
  uso incorrecto
guarantee period
  período de garantía
unit   unidad
opt   optar
initial order
  pedido inicial
sample clock
  reloj de muestra
sales literature
  material
  publicitario
customary habitual,
  de costumbre
comments
  comentarios,
  observaciones

9 April 20..

Martínez Romero, S.L.
Gran Vía, 55
48001 Bilbao
SPAIN

Attention: Mr González Tomás

Dear Mr González

Many thanks for your enquiry of March 20 in which you request us to quote prices, terms and delivery dates for our automatic mains-failure petrol-driven electricity generators.

Before submitting you an offer, however, we would be most grateful if you would provide us with a little more information as regards your exact requirements.

1. What voltage do you wish the generators to produce – 220-240 V or 380 V heavy-duty industrial power?

2. How many operating hours should the generators be able to run for before being refuelled?

3. Where will the generators be located? This is important as far as noise level and insulation are concerned. Our range includes both indoor and outdoor models.

We include our catalogue with this letter to give you an overview of our products and would be pleased to quote you on your exact requirements as soon as we have received the information requested.

Yours sincerely

...

mains-failure
petrol-driven
electricity
generator
generador de electricidad a gasolina en caso de fallo en la red de distribución
heavy-duty
industrial power
energía industrial de gran potencia
operating hour
horas de servicio
refuel repostar
be located estar situado
noise level nivel de ruido
insulation aislamiento
range gama
overview descripción general

AW/wc
19 June 20..

Vidrios Padilla, S.L.
Apartado de Correos 5715
23006 Jaén
SPAIN

Dear Sirs

<u>Order No. LSG/50/03</u>

We hereby confirm your order for laminated security glass as per your fax of 18 June.

We enclose our pro forma invoice as requested and would ask you to notify us as soon as the L/C has been opened. We will then be able to complete your order within a fortnight of receiving confirmation of the documentary credit from our bankers.

We look forward to hearing from you soon.

Yours faithfully
COOK'S GLASS AND GLAZING

Andrew Warmington
Export Manager

laminated security glass vidrio de seguridad laminado
as per de acuerdo con, según
pro forma invoice factura proforma
notify notificar
L/C = letter of credit carta de crédito
complete completar, cumplir
within a fortnight en 15 días, en una quincena
confirmation confirmación
documentary credit crédito documentario

TD/tt
4 July 20..

INTRASHIP LTD
Eastern Dock
Dover DV9 6QY
ENGLAND

Dear Mrs Horrocks

In the course of this week you will be receiving, FOB Dover, 2 containers of electric guitars and amplifiers marked S.W./03 1-2. They are to be shipped on the first available vessel to Rock Nouveau, 16 rue du Général Leclerc, Bayonne, France.
Insurance will be covered by us.

Please make out the B/L to order in triplicate and send all three copies to ourselves. Please also notify us of the name of the vessel as soon as this is known to you.

Yours sincerely
MUSIC AND MORE LTD

Timothy Dearing
Sales Director

electric guitar
  guitarra eléctrica
amplifier
  amplificador
available
  disponible
vessel buque
cover cubrir
make out expedir
B/L = bill of lading
  conocimiento de
  embarque
to order a la orden
in triplicate
  por triplicado
notify notificar,
  informar

Consulta sobre la tarifa de fletes
Enquiry about freight rates

➡ cartas 34, 35

PW/tt
10 November 20..

Specialised Shipping Services
Unit 20
Coppull Trading Estate
Chorley
Lancs PR7 5AY

Dear Sirs

Please quote us your most favourable freight rates
for the transport of 50 tonnes of palletised house
bricks, net weight 1 tonne per unit, for shipment
from Southampton to Tunis in the first two weeks
of December.

Please quote us assuming delivery FOB Southampton stating details of shipping commission and
any further charges.

Yours faithfully
WHALEYS BRICKS LTD

Peter Whaley
Production Manager

quote presupuestar
favourable
 favorable
freight rate
 tarifa de fletes
palletise apilar
brick ladrillo
unit unidad
assume asumir
detail detalle
commission
 comisión
further charges
 gastos adicionales

34 Oferta de flete
Freight Offer

➡ cartas 33, 35

TT/si
15 November 20..

Whaleys Bricks Ltd
28 Mulberry Road
Winchester
WI3 2WW

Dear Mr Whaley

<u>Your Freight Enquiry of 10 November 20..</u>

Thank you for your enquiry regarding the transport of 50 tonnes of palletised house bricks. Our offer is as follows:

> MV CLEETHORPES at £50 per metric tonne or 10 cubic metres, at steamer's option, with 4 lay days

As can be seen from the enclosed sailing card, the vessel is currently located in Marseille and is due to dock in Southampton on November 31st. Loading will commence as from December 1st with an additional charge of £250 for every day of demurrage.

If you accept this offer please forward us the charter party in quadruplicate to enable us to issue the necessary instructions to the ship's captain, Mr Terry Wrigglesworth.

We look forward to your early reply.

Yours sincerely

Theresa Templeton
Specialised Shipping Services

freight enquiry solicitud de flete
at steamer's option opción de buque a vapor *(se refiere aquí a la compañía naviera)*
lay day estadía
sailing card plan de navegación
currently actualmente
dock atracar
load cargar
commence comenzar, iniciar
as from a partir de, desde
additional charge coste adicional
demurrage sobreestadía
forward enviar
charter party póliza de fletamiento
in quadruplicate por cuatriplicado

Aceptación de la oferta de flete
Acceptance of freight offer

➡ cartas 33, 34

35

TW/tt
21 November 20..

Specialised Shipping Services
Unit 20
Coppull Trading Estate
Chorley
Lancs PR7 5AY

Fax: + 44 1524 55057

Dear Ms Templeton

Thank you for your freight offer for palletised house bricks dated 15 November, which we are pleased to accept as follows:

> MV CLEETHORPES at £50 per metric tonne or 10 cubic metres, at steamer's option, with 4 lay days

The consignment of house bricks is from Redland Cement Ltd, Unit 10, Greenfields Industrial Estate, Reading and will be delivered FOB Southampton by Gotruck Haulage Ltd on December 1st.

You will be receiving the charter party in quadruplicate by separate post in the course of this week.

We hope that there will be no reason for delay of any sort and look forward to our order being shipped as agreed.

Yours sincerely
WHALEYS BRICKS LTD

Terry Whaley
Managing Director

palletised house bricks ladrillos paletizados
consignment partida
Industrial Estate zona industrial
by separate post por correo separado
delay demora
of any sort de cualquier tipo

36 Reclamación a la compañía de seguros por avería marítima
Insurance claim after sea-damage

15 June 20..

Lion Assurance Ltd
42 Leadenhall St
London EC1 3ZZ

Dear Sirs

We have just taken delivery of a consignment of 200 bales of raw silk which was insured by yourselves. The merchandise was shipped on S.S. Anastasia, which docked in Plymouth on June 10. When our agents inspected the load they discovered that 15 of the bales were spoiled as a consequence of a storm in the South China Sea (survey report included).

We are therefore placing a claim for the damaged goods with you, the details of which are as follows:

Sea-damage 15 bales
Raw silk £1,000 per bale   £15,000.00
Additional expenses   £48.00
                        Total   £15,048.00

Please arrange to have this sum transferred to our account with the Banco Romeros de Barcelona.

We include all documentation related to this consignment as follows:

1. Insurance certificate
2. Survey report
3. Freight forwarder's invoice
4. Copy of the B/L
5. Ship broker's refusal to grant our claim

We trust you will be able to settle the matter swiftly.

Yours faithfully
...

consignment partida
bale bala, fardo
raw silk seda virgen
merchandise mercancía
load carga
survey report informe de averías
place a claim hacer una reclamación
sea-damage averías por daños marítimos
arrange disponer, tomar las medidas oportunas
related to relacionado con
insurance certificate póliza de seguro
freight forwarder agente de transportes, fletador
B/L = bill of lading conocimiento de embarque
ship broker agente marítimo

➡ carta 38

21 October 20..

Cornwall Plastics Ltd
49 Torrington Road
Penzance
PE3 9IK
Cornwall

Dear Sirs

4,200 KG POLYETHERESTER OF SILICIC ACID

We have duly examined the above mentioned consignment and are pleased to submit our "Clean Report of Findings" to you as follows:

Goods submitted for inspection:	4,200 kg polyester of silicic acid as per pro-forma invoice No. 91900252 dated 1 October 20..
Seller:	Cornwall Plastics Ltd Penzance PE3 9IK, Cornwall, UK
Importer:	Slumberland Foam Inc. 92 Fence Rail Road Pittsburgh Pennsylvania PA49721 USA
FOB value:	US$ 19,812.00
CFR value:	US$ 20,412.00
Country of supply:	Great Britain
Quantity:	20
Packing:	drums
Gross weight:	4,543.00 kg
Net weight:	4,200.00 kg
Marks:	CP/PSA92/1-20

.../2

polyetherester
  poliéster
silicic acid
  ácido silícico
consignment
  partida
report of findings
  informe de
  resultados
submit   presentar
pro-forma invoice
  factura proforma
gross weight
  peso bruto
net weight
  peso neto
mark   marca

FINDINGS

1. Quality: The quality of the goods submitted to us for inspection has been found to comply with the documents presented to us inasmuch as their examination is within our mandate.
2. Quantity: The quantity of goods is as stated above under the rubric "Goods submitted for inspection"
3. Price: Seller's final Invoice No. 0107689 dated 3 October 20.. showing a CFR value of US$ 20412.00 has been submitted to us and we have compared and found acceptable the FOB value of US$ 19849.97 (say ONE NINE EIGHT FOUR NINE POINT NINE SEVEN US DOLLARS)
4. Loading: Scheduled to be shipped at Plymouth on board S.S. Morning Star as per B/L No. D5 dated September 25th 20..

REMARKS

This document is valid only if signed by an authorised representative of Trueworth Ltd and accompanied by the following documents:
- negotiable bill of lading or equivalent evidence of shipment to the USA
- copy of Seller's Final Invoice certified by True-worth Ltd

This "Clean Report of Findings" in no way releases the Sellers from their contractual obligations to the Importers.

Yours faithfully
TRUEWORTH LTD - ASSESSORS
...

comply with
cumplir con
inasmuch as
en tanto que
mandate mandato
rubric título, epígrafe
final invoice
factura final
find acceptable
encontrar aceptable
scheduled
programado
ship embarcar
B/L = bill of lading
conocimiento de embarque
authorised
autorizado
negotiable bill of lading
conocimiento de embarque negociable
certify certificar
release from
liberar de
contractual obligation
obligación contractual
obligation to
obligación para

El agente de transportes confirma el pedido
Freight forwarder confirms order

➡ carta 37

Intertrans Ltd
Units 2 – 10
Marine Walk
Plymouth
PL1 4RF

Our ref: 0123/34218Z
12 January 20..

Cornwall Plastics Ltd
49 Torrington Road
Penzance
Cornwall PE3 9IK

Dear Sirs

We are pleased to confirm that your shipping and on-carriage instructions regarding the consignment mentioned below will be complied with as requested.

The documentation relating to the consignment will be forwarded to you in accordance with your wishes as stated in our previous correspondence.

Consignor:	Cornwall Plastics Ltd
	49 Torrington Road
	Penzance
	PE3 9IK
	Cornwall
Consignee:	Slumberland Foam Inc.
	92 Fence Rail Road
	Pittsburgh
	Pennsylvania PA49721
	USA
Consignment:	2,400 kg (20 drums) polyester of silicic acid

...../2

shipping instructions
instrucciones de embarque
on-carriage instructions
instrucciones de transporte ulterior
consignment
remesa
comply with
atenerse a, cumplir con
relating to
relacionado con
forward enviar
in accordance with
de conformidad con, de acuerdo con
consignor
expedidor, consignatario
consignee receptor, consignado
silicic acid
ácido silícico

Marks:	CP/PSA92/1-20
Total weight:	4,543.00 kg
Shipped on:	10 January 20..
Vessel:	M.S. Morning Star
Destination:	Pittsburgh, Pennsylvania, USA

Should any delay arise or any change in procedure prove necessary, we will notify you as appropriate.

Assuring you of our best attention at all times

Yours faithfully
INTERTRANS LTD

Philip Jones
Manager

cc: Thomas Branscope
    Industrial Shipments Dept.

mark   marca
vessel   buque
MS = motorship
  buque, barco de
  motor
destination
  destino
delay   demora
arise   surgir
procedure
  procedimiento
prove necessary
  verificar que
  es necesario
notify   notificar
as appropriate
  como corresponde

Confirmación de pedido
Confirmation of order

10 August 20..

Perales Exportación, S.L.
Rambla, 138
03002 Alicante
SPAIN

Gentlemen:

Your Order of July 30

Thank you for the above-mentioned order for
500 3.5″ Superlite Disk-Boxes as described in
the August edition of Chip-Talk USA.

We have mailed the merchandise to you by surface
mail and debited $960 to your account as stated.
We expect the goods to arrive by the end of the
month.

We look forward to the pleasure of doing further
business with you in the near future.

Sincerely yours,

Marvin J. Wallis
Export Sales

as described
  según lo descrito
edition edición
mail enviar
  (por correo)
merchandise
  mercancía(s)
surface mail
  aquí: correo
  marítimo
debit adeudar

40 El agente de transportes solicita documentos para el despacho de aduanas

Freight forwarder requests documents for custom clearance

➡ cartas 41–47

EUROFREIGHT LTD
49 Tenterlowe Lane
Hillingdon
Middlesex MU8 8DE

AG/MM
24 March 20..

Glaxo Chemicals Ltd
237 Sutton Common Road
London SW11 3BY

Dear Sirs

Export Consignment to Budapest, Hungary

We refer to the following shipping order:

Consignee:	Budapesti Vegyi Müvek Budapest XII Radnoti Miklos Utca 23 1367 Magyarorszag (Hungary)
Consignment:	10,565 kg bitumen (15 drums) (value £13,300)
Order No.:	191/1.03 (as per your fax of 12 March 20..)
Delivery:	3–4 weeks after receipt of L/C
Hauliers:	Ungarocamion, Budapest

Your customer, Budapesti Vegyi Müvek, has re-quested us to collect the above consignment using Ungarocamion hauliers and forward it in accord-ance with his instructions to Hungary.

...../2

consignement remesa
shipping order *aquí:* orden de embarque
consignee receptor, consignado
delivery entrega
L/C = letter of credit carta de crédito
haulier agencia de transportes (por carretera)

Please therefore let us have details of either the L/C or the documentary collection (B/E, Bs/L) agreed, to enable us to progress forwarding arrangements and issue a forwarder's receipt.

For customs clearance we require:

<u>For Export</u>

• Export notificaton or export declaration

<u>For Import into Hungary</u>

• Commercial Invoice in triplicate
• Packing specification in triplicate

Should you require any further details or information please do not hesitate to call us on 0181 580 4971 or fax us on 0181 580 4862.

Yours faithfully
EUROFREIGHT LTD

Arnold Graham
Transport Controller

documentary collection documentos de cobro
B/E = bill of exchange letra de cambio
Bs/L = bills of lading conocimientos de embarque
progress avanzar
forwarding arrangement convenio de expedición
issue emitir
forwarder's receipt albarán del transportista
customs clearance despacho de aduanas
export notification certificado de exportación
hesitate dudar de

41 Confirmación de recepción de la orden de cobro
Confirmation of receipt of collection order

➡ cartas 40, 42–47

Benson Bank plc
6 Feather Lane
London
EC2 7HK

Our ref.: ATX 4977124
20 February 20..

Glaxo Chemicals Ltd
237 Sutton Common Road
London
SW11 3BY

Dear Sirs

We confirm receipt of the documents listed below for collection. Collection will be in accordance with your instructions and subject to our General Terms of Trade.

| Your ref.: | ZBD Mr Johnson 0078911 |
| Our ref.: | ATX 4977124 |

Drawee:	Budapesti Vegyi Müvek
	Budapest XII
	Radnoti Miklos Utca 23
	1367
	Magyarorszag (Hungary)

Collecting Bank:	Hungarian Business Bank
	Foreign Trade Section
	Szabadsag Ter 8
	1850 Budapest
	Hungary

| Payment: | at sight |
| Amount: | £13,300 + our charges |

...../2

collection cobro
in accordance with de acuerdo con
subject to sujeto a
drawee librado
collecting bank banco de cobro
Foreign Trade Section Sección o Departamento de Comercio Exterior
payment at sight pago a la vista
amount importe
charges gastos

Documents: Commercial Invoice 5/5
Forwarder's receipt 1/1
Certificate of origin 1/1
Certificate of analysis 1/1
Bill of exchange 1/1

This confirmation of receipt is also a copy of our collection order. Please notify us immediately in the event of discrepancies.

Yours faithfully
BENSON BANK PLC

Terence Hill
Foreign Trade Section

Encs

commercial invoice
factura comercial
forwarder's receipt
albarán del
transportista
certificate of origin
certificado de
origen
**certificate of
analysis**
certificado
de análisis
bill of exchange
letra de cambio
discrepancy
discrepancia

42 Orden de cobro
Collection order

➡ cartas 40, 41, 43 – 47

1 March 20..

Hungarian Business Bank
Foreign Trade Section
Szabadsag Ter 8
1850 Budapest
Hungary

Dear Sirs

We enclose the documents listed below for collection:

Commercial invoice	5/5
Forwarder's receipt	1/1
Certificate of origin	1/1
Certificate of analysis	1/1
Bill of exchange	1/1

The above-mentioned is in respect of a consignment of 15 drums of bitumen (value £13,300) to be shipped on March 8, 20.. from London to Budapest. Delivery of the goods is to be taken by the drawee.

Please release the documents on payment of the draft and arrange to have the proceeds of the transaction by SWIFT or by airmail to our Lombard Street branch quoting reference No. ATX 4977124.

Please confirm receipt by SWIFT or on the enclosed form. In the event of non-payment please advise us by SWIFT or, should this not be possible, by airmail.

This order is subject to the "Uniform Rules for Collections" (1995 revision) International Chamber of Commerce Publication No. 522.

Yours faithfully
BENSON BANK PLC
...

commercial invoice factura comercial
forwarder's receipt albarán del transportista
certificate of origin certificado de origen
bill of exchange letra de cambio
drawee librado
draft letra de cambio
SWIFT = Society for Worldwide Interbank Financial Telecommunication Sistema computarizado bancario para transferencias internacionales
Uniform Rules for Collections reglas generales de cobro
International Chamber of Commerce Cámara de Comercio Internacional

Reclamación por daños a mercancías en tránsito
Complaint about damage to goods in transit

➡ cartas 40–42, 44–47

FACSIMILE COVER SHEET	
BUDAPESTI VEGYI MÜVEK	
From: Georg Zold Goods Inwards	To: Mr Terence Stamp Export Sales Manager Glaxo Chemicals Ltd London SW11 3BY ENGLAND
Fax No.: 01 6689	Fax No.: 0181 990 6752
Our ref.: UNG/009.02	Your ref.:
Date: 20 April 20..	No. of pages to follow: 4

**Facsimile
Cover Sheet**
portada de fax

20 April 20..

Dear Mr Stamp

10,565 kg bitumen (15 drums)

We took delivery of the above-mentioned consignment yesterday (19 April) and regret to inform you that 3 of the drums are badly dented with some leakage having occurred. We enclose photographs of the damage for your information and our insurance agent's survey report.

We suspect that the damage was caused in transit and would be grateful if you would arrange for

.../2

above-mentioned
arriba mencionado
be dented
estar abollado
leakage fuga
occur suceder,
producirse
survey report
informe de averías
suspect sospechar
in transit
en tránsito
arrange for
encargarse de

replacements to be sent to us – carriage and insurance paid – by the end of the month when the entire consignment is due to be collected and taken to Siberia by our CIS customer.

This is a new customer with whom we hope to develop a substantial volume of business in the future. For this reason we are very concerned that the agreed timetable should not be changed.

We trust this matter can be settled swiftly and expect the replacement drums to arrive in good time to be forwarded.

Yours sincerely
Budapesti Vegyi Müvek

Georg Zold
Goods Inwards

Encs

replacement
reposición,
recambio
carriage   flete
insurance
seguro
be due
estar previsto
CIS   CEI =
Comunidad
de Estados
Independientes
settle   arreglar
in good time
con tiempo
to be forwarded
ser enviado, ser
expedido

Caso de reclamación de un cliente
al agente de transportes
Referral of customer complaint to freight forwarder

44

➡ cartas 40–43,
45–47

Your ref.: UNG/009.02
Our ref.: TS/tt

21 April 20..

Budapesti Vegyi Müvek
Budapest XII
Radnoti Miklos Utca 23
1367
Hungary

Dear Mr Zold

<u>15 Drums of Bitumen (10,565 kg)</u>

Thank you for your fax dated 20 April in which you refer to damage and leakage in the case of 3 of the drums delivered.

We would point out, however, that according to the forwarder's receipt all 15 drums were accepted for delivery in good order and can therefore only conclude that the damage occurred in transit whilst the goods were in the custody of Eurofreight Ltd, the haulage company. We therefore suggest you contact Eurofreight Ltd, who, in the light of our previous dealings with this company, will undoubtedly settle the matter swiftly and amicably.

As soon as liability has been established we will supply appropriate replacements. Alternatively, we are willing to despatch replacements immediately, carriage forward. Should you wish us to do so please fax us to this effect.

Yours sincerely
GLAXO CHEMICALS LTD

Terence Stamp
Export Sales Manager

damage daño
leakage fuga
forwarder's receipt
  albarán del
  transportista
in good order
  en buen estado
be in the custody of
  estar bajo la
  custodia de
haulage company
  compañía de
  transportes
in the light of
  en vista de
swiftly con rapidez
amicably
  amigablemente
liability
  responsabilidad
establish
  establecer
carriage forward
  porte debido
to this effect
  al respecto,
  en este sentido

45

Reclamación por daños durante el tiempo de tránsito
Complaint about damage in transit

➡ cartas 40–44, 46, 47

Our ref.: UNG/009.02.1
28 April 20..

Eurofreight Ltd
49 Tenterlowe Lane
Hillingdon
Middlesex
MU8 8DE
ENGLAND

Dear Sirs

15 Drums of Bitumen (10,565 kg)

We took delivery of the above-mentioned consignment on 19 April and note that 3 drums are
damaged with leakage. Our suppliers, Glaxo Ltd,
waive liability and claim that the goods were
delivered to yourselves in good condition, as
evidenced by the carrier's receipt. We therefore
have no alternative but to hold you responsible for
the damage, which obviously occurred in transit.
We include a copy of the insurance agent's report
and photographs of the drums for your information.

Glaxo are prepared to supply us with replacements
at short notice - carriage forward - in order to enable us to meet our commitments to our customer
here. We have instructed them to supply us with
3 more drums and will forward the invoice to
yourselves for payment.

We trust this matter will be solved to our mutual
satisfaction.

Yours faithfully
BUDAPESTI VEGYI MÜVEK
...

consignment
remesa
waive liability
eximir de una
responsabilidad
in good condition
en buenas
condiciones
evidenced
probado
carrier's receipt
albarán del
transportista
have no alternative
but no tener otra
alternativa que
hold s.o.
responsible
responsabilizar
a alguien
insurance agent
agente de seguros
at short notice
en breve
to meet one's
commitments
cumplir con sus
obligaciones
to our mutual
satisfaction para
satisfacción de ambos

Reclamación de un cliente a la compañía de seguros
Referral of customer complaint to insurance company

➡ cartas 40–45, 47

Your ref.: UNG/009.02.1
5 May 20..

Budapesti Vegyi Müvek
Budapest XII
Radnoti Miklos Utca 23
1367
HUNGARY

Dear Mr Zold

Thank your for your letter of 28 April in which you give details of damage to 3 drums of bitumen delivered by ourselves to your company on April 19th. We regret the inconvenience caused and feel you acted correctly by having the damage assessed by your insurance agent.

We have looked into the matter and examined the driver's log for the trip in question and have discovered that our vehicle was involved in a minor accident. The case is currently in the hands of our lawyers and should be settled by the end of the month. Our insurance cover provides for indemnification for any eventuality so we would therefore request you to approach our insurers, whose name and address are as follows:

Accident Insurance Europe
Insurance House
London EC1A 4WW
England

Please quote policy No. GLX/342-00/03.

We trust the matter will be settled to your satisfaction in due course.

Yours sincerely
EUROFREIGHT LTD
...

inconvenience
  molestias
act correctly
  actuar
  correctamente
have the damage
  assessed haber
  valorado los daños
look into the matter
  estudiar el
  problema
log libro de ruta
vehicle vehículo
be involved
  estar involucrado
lawyer
  abogado
insurance cover
  cobertura
  del seguro
indemnification
  indemnización
eventuality
  incidentes
approach
  dirigirse a
policy póliza

47 Reclamación a la agencia de seguros
Making an insurance claim

➡ cartas 40–46

Budapesti Vegyi Müvek
Budapest XII
Radnoti Miklos Utca 23
1367
Hungary

Policy No.: GLX/342-00/03.
14 May 20..

Insurance Accident Europe
Insurance House
London EC1A 4WW
ENGLAND

Dear Sirs

15 Drums of Bitumen (10,565 kg)

We took delivery of the above-mentioned consignment on 19 April and regret to inform you that 3 of the drums are badly dented with some leakage having occurred. We enclose photographs of the damage for your information and our insurance agent's survey report.

We have so far approached both Glaxo Chemicals Ltd, the suppliers, and Eurofreight Ltd, the haulage company, and as neither of these parties will accept liability we are turning to you on the advice of Eurofreight Ltd to claim compensation.

Please refer to the enclosed insurance agent's survey report for details of the damage and an assessment of the replacement costs. We also enclose copies of all documentation authenticated by the British Consulate in Budapest.

We trust you will send us the necessary claims forms at your earliest convenience to ensure that this matter is settled once and for all.

.../2

insurance agent
   agente de seguros
survey report
   informe de averías
supplier   proveedor
accept liability
   aceptar la
   responsabilidad
on the advice of
   por recomendación
   de
claim compensation
   reclamar
   compensación
replacement
   reposición
authenticate
   certificar,
   autentificar
claim form
   formulario de
   reclamación
ensure   asegurar,
   garantizar
once and for all
   de una vez por todas

We have already incurred losses because of this situation and reserve the right to make a claim for them.

We also wish to point out that, should we incur further losses as a result of our customer's cancelling the order owing to delay in delivery, we will also claim compensation for loss of business.

We look forward to your early reply in this matter.

Yours faithfully
BUDAPESTI VEGYI MÜVEK

Georg Zold
Goods Inwards

Encs

incur further losses
sufrir más pérdidas, sufrir pérdidas adicionales
cancel the order
cancelar el pedido
delay in delivery
demora en la entrega
loss of business
pérdida de negocio

15 May 20..

JMJ Engineering
89 Brocks Drive
East Cheam
London SW14 1UZ
ENGLAND

Dear Mr Marshall

Our Order No. 342/03 for Piston Rings

In order to obtain an import licence for the items ordered and to open the L/C, we require a pro forma invoice containing price estimates and quantities.

We would be obliged if you would send us this by the end of the month to enable us to effect delivery as soon as possible.

Yours sincerely
MAQUINARIA SÁNCHEZ, S.L.

José Águila
Purchasing Manager

piston ring anillo de pistón
import licence licencia de importación
item artículo
L/C = letter of credit carta de crédito
estimate estimación
effect delivery efectuar el envío
Purchasing Manager Director de Compras

Solicitud de emisión de una factura aduanera
Request for a customs invoice to be issued

AT/gh
27 April 20..

New Form Plastics Moulds Ltd
Unit 19
Needham Industrial Estate
Oxford
OX8 7HH
ENGLAND

Dear Sirs

As the value of the plastics moulds ordered by
ourselves in our letter of February 28 exceeds
£50,000 sterling, we require a customs invoice
for the customs authorities here to enable them
to assess import duty. We would therefore be most
grateful if you would issue this document at your
earliest convenience to enable us to complete the
necessary formalities at this end.

Yours faithfully
MUTUMBUKO PLASTICS LTD

Arnold Twumasi
Import Manager

plastic mould
  molde de plástico
exceed   sobrepasar,
  superar
customs invoice
  factura de aduanas
customs authority
  autoridades
  aduaneras
to assess   gravar
import duty
  aranceles
**at your earliest
  convenience**
  a la mayor
  brevedad posible
formality
  formalidad
at this end
  aquí: por nuestra
  parte

50 Solicitud de cuenta abierta con un proveedor
Requesting open account payment terms with a supplier

➡ carta 51

JT/gg
29 March 20..

C. & W. Berry Industrial Paints
Wellford Mill Lane
Leyland
Preston PR5 1LE

Dear Mr Berry

Further to our recent telephone call regarding the supply of industrial paints for our retail outlets throughout the UK, I am pleased to advise you that we are prepared to stock your products for a trial period of 90 days as from the beginning of April.

We feel, for the time being, that open account terms with regular quarterly statements would be most appropriate.

Please invoice us here at Head Office in Manchester for all deliveries to all outlets itemising the goods supplied to show unit and total prices and indicating which of our branches have been supplied.

We trust this arrangement will prove satisfactory and would be pleased to receive written confirmation by mail or fax by return.

Yours sincerely
THE CROWN TRADE CENTRE

John Tidmarsh
Head Buyer

industrial paint
pintura industrial
retail outlet
minorista
stock almacenar
trial period
período de prueba
open account terms
pago a través de
cuenta abierta
quarterly statement
extracto trimestral
invoice facturar
Head Office
oficina central
itemise detallar,
desglosar
unit price
precio unitario
total price
precio total
Head Buyer
Jefe de Compras

Pago de facturas (envío de extracto)
Settlement of account (sending a statement)

➡ carta 50

WB/js
2 July 20..

THE CROWN TRADE CENTRE
23–41 Gresham Road
Manchester MA4 1HQ

Dear Mr Tidmarsh

Please find enclosed our statement of account for the period April 1st – June 30th.

As requested we have itemised all deliveries to include unit and total prices and have indicated which of your stores was supplied in each case.

We have deducted £47.92 from the price of the consignment of "Dawn Beige Coverplus Vinyl" delivered to your Preston branch on June 23rd owing to the poor shade match with the previous batch. We trust this will prove acceptable to you.

Please pay by transfer to our account with the Newtown Bank in Manchester (Account No. 2346731).

We look forward to doing further business with you and remain

Yours sincerely
C. & W. BERRY INDUSTRIAL PAINTS

William Berry
Co-director

Enc

**statement
 of account** extracto de cuenta
deduct deducir
consignment remesa
branch sucursal, filial
owing to debido a
shade matiz, tono
match *aquí:* en concordancia con
batch remesa, lote
acceptable aceptable
pay by transfer pagar a través de transferencia

52

Pago a través de transferencia bancaria (SWIFT)
Payment by bank transfer (SWIFT)

IG/po
26 June 20..

Benson Bank plc
34–38 Market Place
New Malden
Surrey KT3 5TZ

Dear Sir

<u>Our Account No. 789315</u>

Please transfer the sum of

£5,423.00

to the account of Subirá Ortiz Publicidad, S.L. in
Madrid, Spain in respect of their invoice No.
02/4/EXTR./4093.

The account details are as follows:
Account holder: Subirá Ortiz Publicidad
Account No.:   789046001
Branch Code: 45240056

We would be grateful if you would arrange for
payment to be effected by SWIFT to ensure that
the funds arrive by the end of the month.

Yours faithfully
VANTAGE ADVERTISING

Iain Gowe
European Campaigns Manager

transfer transferir
account cuenta
in respect of
  con relación a
detail detalle
account holder
  titular de la cuenta
branch code
  código de la
  sucursal
arrange for
  disponer
effect efectuar
ensure asegurar
funds fondos

➡ cartas
54–57

AL/gl
12 July 20..

Óptica Ortiz Díaz, S.A.
c/ Botella, 15
28020 Madrid
Spain

Attention: Señor Revilla Bote

Dear Señor Revilla

May we draw your attention to the enclosed brochure containing details of our new multifocal, light-sensitive lenses, which are especially suited for those frequently engaged in outdoor pursuits. We feel that we have "beaten the others past the post" as far as marketing this new, low-price product from the USA is concerned and are sure that it will find a ready market in Spain.

May we also draw your attention to our invoice No. 1892Z/5/01 dated May 1st which, according to our records, is so far unpaid. We feel sure that this is due to an oversight on your part and would appreciate payment within the next few days. If payment has already been effected please disregard this letter.

We look forward to hearing from you soon.

Yours sincerely
NORTHERN OPTICS LTD

Alan Gore
Credit Controller

Enc

brochure folleto
contain details contener detalles
multifocal lense lente u objetivo multifocal
light-sensitive fotosensible
outdoor exterior
pursuit actividad, pasatiempos
to beat the others past the post adelantarse a los demás
low-price a bajo precio
find a ready market tener salida en el mercado
record archivo
oversigth descuido
disregard no hacer caso
optics óptica

54 Segundo aviso
Second reminder

➡ cartas 53, 55–57

AL/gl
10 August 20..

Óptica Ortiz Díaz, S.A.
c/ Botella, 15
28020 Madrid
Spain

Attention: Señor Revilla Bote

Dear Señor Revilla

Your Ref.:   023/499
Account No.:   SO/894377
Balance Due: £4,231.92
Due Date: 15 June 20..

I am disappointed to note that, despite our previous reminder of 12 July, your account with us still remains unpaid. You will recall from our Conditions of Sale that all outstanding balances due to us must be paid within thirty days after receipt of our invoice. By placing an order with us you indicated your agreement to our terms. According to my records no query has been raised with regard to the goods delivered or the accounts rendered.

Under the circumstances I would be grateful if you could arrange for the above sum to be paid by return. Should you fail to do so I shall have no alternative but to add interest to the balance at the rate of 25% per annum as prescribed by our Conditions of Sale.

Yours sincerely
NORTHERN OPTICS LTD

Alan Gore
Credit Controller

balance due   saldo deudor
due date   fecha de vencimiento
conditions of sale condiciones de venta
outstanding balances   saldos pendientes
within 30 days dentro de los 30 días
receipt   recepción
with regard to the accounts rendered con respecto a las facturas/cuentas presentadas
by return a vuelta de correo
interest   interés
at the rate of 25% per annum   a un tipo de interés del 25% anual
as prescribed según lo establecido

Último aviso
Final demand

➡ cartas 53, 54, 56, 57

AL/gl
18 August 20..

Óptica Ortiz Díaz, S.A.
c/ Botella, 15
28020 Madrid
Spain

Attention: Señor Revilla Bote

Dear Señor Revilla

Balance Due: £4,231.92
Interest Accrued: £352.58

Despite repeated reminders your account still remains unpaid. Unless I receive a remittance covering all balances due within four days from the date of this letter I will have no alternative but to instruct our solicitors to take legal action against you.

In this case proceedings will be instigated without further notice to regain the sum owed, the interest accrued for the outstanding period and the costs of legal action.

Yours sincerely
NORTHERN OPTICS LTD

Alan Gore
Credit Controller

interest accrued
 interés devengado
remittance remesa
instruct
 dar instrucciones
solicitor abogado
take legal action
 against you
 emprender acciones
 legales contra usted
proceedings
 medidas,
 procedimientos
instigate
 aquí: iniciar
without further
 notice sin más
 notificación
regain recuperar
costs of legal action
 costes de la
 acción legal

56

Solicitud de ampliación del plazo de la letra
Request for prolongation of draft

FACSIMILE COVER SHEET	
Óptica Ortiz Díaz, S.A.	
From: Carlos Revilla Bote Sales Manager	To: Alan Gore Credit Controller
Fax No.: +91 284 44 01	Fax No.: +1772 20936
Our ref.: 023/499	Your ref.: AL/gl
Date: 2 September 20..	No. of pages to follow: 1

➡ cartas
53–55, 57

Facsimile Cover
Sheet
portada de fax

2 Sept 20..

Dear Mr Gore

Account No. SO/894377
Outstanding Balance

Please forgive us for not replying to your letters
earlier. We have recently undergone a major
restructuring of the company entailing a move to
more suitable premises on the outskirts of Madrid
and a significant rationalisation of staffing levels.
This, in turn, has led to a number of problems in
the Accounts Department, which has now been
entirely re-organised. We are currently dealing with
a considerable backlog of administrative matters
and have, at the same time, been doing our best

.../2

undergo sufrir
restructuring
reestructuración
entail implicar,
suponer
premises local
outskirts
alrededores, afueras
staffing levels
dotación de
personal
**Accounts
Department**
Departamento
de Contabilidad
backlog
acumulación

to keep up with the unexpectedly large influx of advance orders for our new light-sensitive lenses.

We would, under the circumstances, be grateful if you would permit us to prolong the draft until September 30, by which date we will have remitted all monies owing to you including interest accrued.

We trust you will agree to this proposal. You can rest assured that the matter will be settled by the end of the month.

Yours sincerely

Carlos Revilla
Sales Manager

P.S.
Please note the address of our new premises:
c/ de María de Molina, 156, 28006 Madrid, Spain

influx   entrada
light-sensitive
  fotosensible
draft   letra de
  cambio, giro
interest accrued
  interés devengado
proposal
  propuesta

57 El acreedor está dispuesto a aceptar un pago parcial
Creditor prepared to accept part-payment

➡ cartas 53–56

AL/gl
3 September 20..

Óptica Ortiz Díaz, S.A.
c/ de María de Molina, 156
28006 Madrid
Spain

Attention: Señor Revilla

Dear Señor Revilla

Your Account No.:   SO/894377
Total outstanding: £4,584.40

We have received your fax of 2 September.

We find your proposal unacceptable, above all because of the inordinately long period of time that has elapsed since the first of our three reminders (12 July) and your response. This has led us to conclude that you are not interested in maintaining a business relationship with us in the long term.

We are, however, prepared to accept an immediate payment of £2,500 accompanied by a draft drawn on yourselves at 30 d/s for £2,162.75 in respect of the unpaid balance including interest accrued by expiry on October 4th. We enclose our new draft for your acceptance.

Please indicate by return whether you accept these terms or not. Should they prove unacceptable we will immediately initiate proceedings for the recovery of all monies due.

Yours sincerely
NORTHERN OPTICS LTD
...

total outstanding
total pendiente de pago
inordinately
excesivamente
period of time
período de tiempo
elapsed
transcurrido
maintain
mantener
in the long term
a largo plazo
accompanied by
acompañado por
drawn on
extendido a/a nombre de
30 d/s = days/sight
30 días vista
expiry   caducidad, vencimiento
acceptance
aceptación
initiate proceedings
iniciar procedimientos, tomar medidas
recovery
aquí: recuperación

June 17, 20..

Hudson Mechanical Engineering Inc.
782 Fairweather Street
Boston, Massachusetts 02116
USA

Gentlemen:

We received your letter of 10 June and are sorry that there has been a delay in paying your Invoice No. 094/5/02.

We have unfortunately been hit by the economic downswing in Europe as a whole and in the engineering sector in particular, which has resulted in temporary financial difficulties for our company.

A considerable number of our customers have had to file applications for bankruptcy and, pending decisions in these cases, which could go on for months, we are not in a position to press them for payment. We have, nevertheless, been given assurances by our bankers that part-payment of your invoice is possible. We have therefore transferred 50% of the sum outstanding to your account.

With respect to the outstanding balance we are unfortunately compelled to request you to grant us an extension of a further 30 days for this sum. If you can see your way clear to granting us this facility please send us a draft at 30 d/s drawn upon ourselves to this effect, which we will accept and return to you immediately.

We trust you will understand our predicament, which, as you can see, is entirely due to circumstances beyond our control.

Sincerely yours,
...

economic downswing
recesión económica
engineering sector
sector de la ingenieria
file an application for bankruptcy
archivar una solicitud de quiebra
press s.o. for payment insistir a alguien para el pago
outstanding balance
pago pendiente
draft at 30 d/s (days/sight)
giro a 30 días vista
drawn upon ourselves librado a nuestra orden
predicament
aprieto, apuro
be due to circumstances beyond our control
ser debido a circunstancias ajenas a nuestro control

59 Petición de recomendación de un representante
Request for the recommendation of an agent

28 February 20..

South Western Bank plc
Leadenhall Street
London EC1 4WW
England

Dear Sirs

Request for Assistance with Engaging a UK Agent

We are a major Spanish supplier of fitted kitchen equipment with an annual turnover in Spain well in excess of Euros 30 m. We have so far been represented in the UK by Messrs Crowther & Tidmarsh, a firm of kitchen suppliers which has now ceased trading owing to the death of Mr Tidmarsh. It is for this reason that we are turning to you to ask for assistance in finding a suitable agent for our products.

The firm or individual in question would sell on our behalf on a commission basis, preferably through an already existing network of retail outlets throughout the UK and possibly Northern Ireland. We feel that a well-capitalised company would be able to stock a sufficient quantity of our products to give an impression of our wide range.

We would therefore be extremely grateful if you could recommend a suitable company. We would, of course, also be pleased if your bank would handle all payments arising from the business an agency network would generate.

We very much hope that you will be able to assist us in this matter and remain

Yours faithfully
COCINAS GALDO, S.L.
...

fitted kitchen
  cocina integral
annual turnover
  cifra de negocios anual/facturación anual
m = million
  millón
cease trading
  suspender actividades comerciales
on our behalf
  en nuestro nombre
on a commission basis
  en base a una comisión
network   red
retail outlet
  minorista
a well-capitalised company   una compañía solvente
to stock
  aprovisionar, tener en almacén
range   gama
generate   *aquí:* suponer

Solicitud para ser el representante de una empresa
Application to become an agent for a firm

➡ cartas 61-63

Deportes Alonso
Canales, 27
46002 Valencia
Spain

20 March 20..

Land & Hunter Sportswear Specialists
12 Thames Street
Kingston
Surrey KT1 1PF
England

Dear Sirs

Enquiry about Agency Agreement

In their latest information bulletin our bankers, the Banco Regional in Valencia, publicised your request to them for assistance in finding an agent for your sportswear in Spain.

We have a comprehensive network of specialised retail sportswear outlets throughout Valencia and, in addition, have branches in all major Spanish cities. We understand from our bankers that you specialise in durable, waxed cotton clothing, lightweight boots, tents and survival gear. We feel there is excellent potential for such equipment here and, provided the quality is in keeping with our customers' expectations, would welcome an opportunity to market your products in Spain.

We would appreciate it, if you would send us comprehensive sales literature on your products together with a sample tent, waxed cotton anorak and perhaps any other items you feel will show off your goods effectively.

.../2

agency agreement
contrato de representación
publicise
hacer público
sportswear
ropa de deporte
comprehensive
amplio, completo
retail outlet
minorista
branch sucursal
durable duradero
waxed cotton
algodón parafinado/ resinado
survival gear
equipo de supervivencia
sales literature
folleto publicitario/ informativo
sample tent
tienda de campaña de muestra
show off effectively
realzar con eficacia

Should you require references, the Banco Regional in Valencia will be pleased to supply you with any information you may desire.

We feel sure that this could well be the beginning of a successful business venture and look forward to hearing from you in the near future. For your information we enclose a brochure and further details of our organisation.

Yours faithfully
DEPORTES ALONSO

Álvaro Delgado
Managing Director

Enc

successful business venture
cooperación empresarial provechosa

Oferta de representación exclusiva
Offer of sole agency

→ cartas 60, 62, 63

30 March 20..

Deportes Alonso
Canales, 27
46002 Valencia
Spain

Dear Mr Delgado

Sole Agency Agreement

Many thanks for your letter of 20 March, in which you express an interest in marketing our goods.

We are, indeed, looking for an agent for our products in Spain and it sounds as if your organisation could well fit the bill. Our products are tremendously successful over here in the UK. Waxed cotton clothing is now all the rage and the market is expanding fast. We enclose the samples you request together with illustrated sales literature and our latest trade price-list. We feel sure that the quality will give you no grounds for complaint, as our products are truly state-of-the-art and used by top mountaineers throughout the world.

The Banco Regional describes your organisation as sound and efficient and therefore, provided you are satisfied with the samples, all that remains is for our lawyers to draft a sole agency agreement ready for signature.

We suggest a meeting here in Kingston to sign the agreement and to get to know each other a little better.

Yours sincerely
LAND & HUNTER

...

sole agency agreement contrato de representación exclusiva
fit the bill ser apropiado/apto
be tremendously successful tener gran éxito
waxed cotton algodón parafinado/ resinado
be all the rage hacer furor
sample muestra
illustrated sales literature folletos ilustrados/ informativos
trade price-list lista de precios al por mayor
give no grounds for complaint no dar motivos para reclamaciones
state-of-the-art el último modelo, lo más novedoso
sound sólido
to draft an agreement redactar un contrato

62

Confirmación de la oferta de representación en exclusiva
Confirmation of sole agency offer

➡ cartas 60, 61, 63

Deportes Alonso
Canales, 27
46002 Valencia
Spain

15 May 20..

Land & Hunter Sportswear Specialists
12 Thames Street
Kingston
Surrey KT1 1PF
England

Dear Mr Land

Confirmation of Agency

After our very instructive and positive meeting in Kingston we should like to state once again the main points upon which we reached agreement as regards our future co-operation:

1. We are to act as your sole agents in Spain for the agreed period.

2. The conditions stated in the agreement are valid for a period of two years after the date of the agreement.

3. We undertake to trade with no imported products of a similar nature which could compete with the products to which this agreement relates.

4. Account sales will be submitted quarterly and we will accept your drafts on us for the net amount accruing from sales of your products.

instructive
  instructivo
reach agreement
  ponerse de acuerdo
sole agent
  representante
  exclusivo
undertake
  comprometerse a
compete   competir
account sales
  aquí: liquidación
  de ventas
submit   presentar
quarterly
  trimestralmente
draft   giro, letra
on us   nominales
accrue   acumular

...../2

5. We undertake to display a representative cross-section of your products in all of our retail outlets in Spain in such a manner as to bring them to the attention of a maximum number of customers.

We trust that you will send us written confirmation of these points in due course and look forward to receiving your draft of the agency agreement.

The final version will need to be translated into Spain, but that is something which we can organise here in Valencia.

Yours sincerely
DEPORTES ALONSO

Álvaro Delgado
Managing Director

cross-section
  muestra
  representativa
retail outlet
  mercado al
  por menor
in due course
  a su debido tiempo
agency agreement
  acuerdo de
  representación

63 Informe del representante
Agent's report

➡ cartas 60, 61, 62

Deportes Alonso
Canales, 27
46002 Valencia
Spain

1 November 20..

Land & Hunter Sportswear Specialists
12 Thames Street
Kingston
Surrey KT1 1PF
England

Dear Mr Land

<u>Report on First Quarter Sales</u>

We are pleased to inform you that sales activity has been brisk throughout this first quarter with a balance of 34,000 euros in your favour. On presentation of your draft drawn on us for this amount of 30 d/s it will be accepted and returned to you immediately, as agreed.

We feel that our advertising campaign, launched as it was at the end of the summer season, was particularly effective because waxed cotton jackets are most suited to weather conditions at this time of year. The new Spanish TV series bought from Thames Televison entitled "Outdoor Style" featuring prominent British TV personalities wearing your company's anoraks has also certainly had a beneficial effect on sales. We enclose some material from the advertising campaign and press coverage of the TV series for your information.

For the next quarter we expect an even greater turnover, particularly in the bigger men's sizes with

.../2

first quarter sales ventas del primer trimestre
brisk animado, activo
balance in your favour saldo a su favor
on presentation a la presentación
draft giro, letra
advertising campaign campaña de publicidad
waxed cotton algodón parafinado/resinado
feature enseñar, mostrar
beneficial beneficioso
sales ventas
turnover facturación

large waist measurements. Please make sure that these sizes are available in greater numbers to accommodate the market here.

As regards pricing policy, we feel that the current weakness of the pound should be passed on to our customers and suggest an across-the-board price reduction of 10% on the trade prices quoted.

We look forward to your comments on this matter and are confident that the market will continue to offer considerable potential for the foreseeable future.

Yours sincerely
DEPORTES ALONSO

Álvaro Delgado
Managing Director

Encs

waist measurement
  talla de cintura
accommodate
  satisfacer
pricing policy
  política de precios
across-the-board
  global
trade price precio
  al por mayor
potential potencial
foreseeable future
  futuro previsible

64 Consulta sobre precios de seguros
Enquiry about insurance rates

➡ cartas 65, 66

5 April 20..

Sovereign Assurance Ltd
London Regional Marine Branch
24 Lime Street
London EC3 7JE

Dear Sir or Madam

Please let us have your quotation for insurance cover against all risks, warehouse to warehouse, for a consignment of:

50 bales of raw silk from Liverpool to Marseille on board the vessel "MS Northern Star" of the M&P Line.

Replacement value is £5,000.

Cover is required as from June 1st.

Yours faithfully
Turnpike Trading Co. Ltd

Ronald Soames
Director

quotation
  cotización
insurance cover
  cobertura del
  seguro
warehouse
  almacén
consignment
  partida
bale bala, fardo
raw silk seda
  virgen
replacement value
  valor de reposición
as from desde

Cuota de seguro
Insurance quotation

65

➡ cartas 64, 66

10 April 20..

Turnpike Trading Co. Ltd
Unit 5
Watery Lane Trading State
Gunnerbury
Middlesex MI5 3TH

Dear Sirs

Thank you for your letter of 5 April, in which you
ask for our quotation for:

Risk:	50 bales of raw silk, Liverpool – Marseille
Vessel:	MS Northern Star
Shipping company:	M&P Line
Value:	£5,000
Cover:	all risks, warehouse to warehouse
Dates:	as from 1 June 20..

We are pleased to quote you as follows:

15%

This offer is subject to the silk being seaworthily
packed.

We look forward to your reply to this quotation
and remain

Yours faithfully
SOVEREIGN ASSURANCE LTD
...

risk riesgo
bale bala, fardo
raw silk
  seda virgen
vessel buque
shipping company
  compañía naviera
value valor
cover cobertura
be subject to
  estar sujeto a
be seaworthily
  packed embalado
  debidamente para
  el transporte
  marítimo
quotation cuota,
  presupuesto

103

66 Aceptación de las condiciones del seguro
Taking out insurance cover

➡ cartas 64, 65

20 April 20..

Sovereign Assurance Ltd
London Regional Marine Branch
24 Line Street
London EC3 7JE

Dear Sirs

Thank you for your quotation of 10 April for warehouse to warehouse cover for a consignment of 50 bales of raw silk from Liverpool to Marseille to be shipped on or after June 1st.

We are pleased to accept your quotation and would request you to forward the necessary documents to us for the policy to be signed.

We have taken note of your stipulation that seaworthy packing is necessary and will ensure that this is provided.

Yours faithfully
Turnpike Trading Co. Ltd

Ronald Soames
Director

consignment
 remesa
on or after
 en o después de
quotation
 aquí: información
 sobre cuotas
policy póliza
take note of
 tomar nota de
stipulation
 estipulación
seaworthy packing
 embalaje debido
 para el transporte
 marítimo
ensure asegurar
provide
 proporcionar

104

Renovación de una póliza flotante
Renewal of floating policy

15 May 20..

Pacific European Timber Export Ltd
White Cross
Cameron House
Lancaster
LA4 T76

Dear Sirs

Renewal of Floating Policy No. 896/3/02

Thank you for your letter of May 10th in which
you request the above-mentioned floating policy
covering shipments of timber from Singapore
to UK ports be renewed.

We hereby confirm that warehouse to warehouse
cover has once again been provided for by ourselves to the value of £40,000.

Yours faithfully
CONDOR INSURANCE (UK) LTD

Ralf Barrow
Commercial Policies Division

shipment
 embarque
timber   madera
renew   renovar
to the value of
 por el valor de
**Commercial
 Policies Division**
 División de Pólizas
 Comerciales

12 March 20..

Messrs Porter & Jones
Solicitors
41 Leadbetter Lane
London EC3 9PP

Dear Sirs

We have pleasure in informing you, as valued customers of long standing, that "Infotec", which has hitherto traded as a sole proprietorship will, as from June 1st of this year, commence trading as a private limited company under the name, "Infotec Ltd".

You may rest assured that the high standard of personal attention and consultancy afforded to our customers in the past will be maintained and, indeed, underpinned by a broader spread of expertise and experience.

Enclosed you will find our "Customer Services" brochure itemising our enhanced range of services and providing biographical details of the new co-directors we have been fortunate enough to have join us.

Please do not hesitate to contact us should you have any queries as regards your firm's requirements or any other matter of concern.

All service contracts extending beyond May 31st will be amended to include the company under its new name and forwarded to our customers for signature.

We look forward to the pleasure of serving you soon.

Yours faithfully
INFOTEC
...

valued customer apreciado cliente
of long standing desde hace tiempo
hitherto hasta la fecha
sole proprietorship empresa de un solo propietario
private limited company (Ltd) sociedad limitada (GB)
rest assured tener la seguridad de que
underpin apuntalar
a broader spread un más amplio despliegue
expertise variedad de servicios
itemise detallar, especificar
range of services gama de servicios
biographical details detalles biográficos
service contract contrato de servicios

Britannia Rock Building Society
24–26 Old Cattle Market
Manchester
MA6 7BR

15 April 20..

Mr & Mrs William Galsworthy
42 Acacia Avenue
Rotherham
RO1 4IK
Lancashire

Dear Mr and Mrs Galsworthy

Opening of a New Branch

We have great pleasure in announcing that we shall shortly be opening a new branch of the *Britannia Rock Building Society* within easy reach of your home address.

We are now handling such a large volume of accounts in the north of England that it has proved necessary to expand our activities to cope with the ever-increasing demand for our services.

The new Branch Manager in Rotherham, Mr Terence Birchall, has had many years experience in the field of property acquisition and finance and would welcome an opportunity to meet you personally. He would therefore like to invite you to the new branch's open day on Monday, May 1st between 10 a.m. and 3.30 p.m. when the *Britannia Rock* will be pleased to extend its hospitality to all visitors caring to participate in light refreshment.

.../2

branch   sucursal
within easy reach
  muy cerca de
handle   manejar
volume   volumen
account   cuenta
prove necessary
  demostrar la
  necesidad
ever-increasing
  demand   demanda
  en constante
  aumento
Branch Manager
  Director de
  Sucursal
property acquisition
  adquisición de
  propiedades
hospitality
  hospitalidad
participate
  participar

Our Head Office in Manchester, which currently holds your account, will be sending you our "New Option" form, which will enable you to transfer your account to the Rotherham Branch with a minimum of formalities, should you so wish. Customers opting to retain their account in Manchester are, of course, at liberty to do so. The choice is entirely up to you. For your information we enclose details of some of the new services which will be available at all our branches from the autumn of this year.

We look forward to meeting you in May and would also like to take this opportunity to thank you for the trust you have placed in us in the past.

Yours sincerely
BRITANNIA ROCK BUILDING SOCIETY

Hardy Winter
Chief Executive

Enc

hold an account
  llevar una cuenta
transfer transferir
formality
  formalidad
opt optar
retain mantener
be at liberty to
  do s.th. tener
  la libertad de
  hacer algo

Cambio de dirección de una empresa
Change of firm's address

21 July 20..

Harvard Plastics Ltd
100–110 Heavytree Lane
Penzance PE2 6ZZ
Cornwall

Dear Sir or Madam

Please note that our firm will be trading from a new address as from August 15 and address all future correspondence to:

Trelawney Plastic Moulds Ltd
Units 1–4
Rusholm Bridge Trading Estate
Penzance PE2 8PU

Our telephone and fax numbers remain unchanged.

Yours faithfully

P. J. O'Sullivan (Ms)
Communications Manager

note *aquí:* tomar nota
trade hacer negocios
plastic mould molde de plástico
trading estate immueble comercial
remain unchanged permanecer invariable

71 Cierre de un negocio
Closing down a business

1 February 20..

Southall Groceries
42 Clarence Parade
Southall
Middlesex MX3 6ZZ

Dear Sirs

It is our sad duty to inform you that for personal reasons The Hackney Trading Company Ltd will be dissolved as from June 1st. This is due to the fact that the principal shareholder and director, Mr Terence Newbury, will be retiring at the end of May and the other members are, for personal reasons, not in a position to take over the running of the company.

The company will be dissolved in the customary manner as prescribed by the Companies Acts with Mr Terence Newbury acting as liquidator for a period of one year.

All outstanding orders will be executed in accordance with existing contracts.

New orders can be placed until March 31 of this year.

We wish to take this opportunity to thank you for the loyalty you have shown towards our company and assure you that we will also be pleased to answer any queries you may have regarding your contracts or any other matters arising.

Yours faithfully
THE HACKNEY TRADING COMPANY LTD
...

dissolve disolver
principal shareholder principal accionista
retire jubilar
running *aquí:* funcionamiento, marcha
customary habitual
prescribe prescribir, ordenar
Companies Act ley británica de sociedades mercantiles
liquidator interventor
outstanding order pedido pendiente de entrega
existing contract contrato vigente
loyalty lealtad
arise surgir, presentarse

➡ carta 73

15th June 20..

The Manager
Air Space Freight Forwarding
100 Thornbury Road
Newcastle
England

Dear Sir or Madam

I am writing in reply to your advertisement in the European News of June 12th for the post of Sales Manager in your European Division.

I am aged 27, of Spanish nationality, single, bilingual Spanish/English and am currently employed as Freight Co-ordinator with Quick Express España in Madrid where I am responsible for freight movements to and from the US and the UK. I have held this post for three years now and would welcome an opportunity to work in Britain.

I now have a total of 5 years' work experience in freight forwarding, having completed a 2 1/2-year training course as a freight forwarder with Morales Sánchez, Madrid where I stayed for a further two years after completing my training period before taking up my current post at Quick Express. My current performance-related salary is in excess of £30K p.a.

I enclose a full curriculum vitae and the names of two referees as stipulated.

I look forward to your reply at your earliest convenience.

Yours faithfully
...

Sales Manager
   Director de Ventas
nationality
   nacionalidad
**Freight
   Co-ordinator**
   Coordinador
   de Transportes
freight movement
   tráfico de
   mercancía(s)
**welcome an
   opportunity**
   agradecer una
   oportunidad
freight forwarding
   expedición de
   mercancías
freight forwarder
   agente de
   transportes
**performance-
   related**   pago
   según rendimiento
£ 30K p. a.
   30.000 Libras
   Esterlinas anuales
   (K = 1.000)
referee   *aquí:*
   persona que puede
   dar referencias
stipulate   estipular

73 Invitación a una entrevista
Invitation to an interview

➡ carta 72

21 June 20..

Jaime Otero Lugo
Calle de la Sal, 5, 2°
28028 Madrid
Spain

Dear Mr Otero

Thank you for your letter of 15 June in which you submit your application for the post of European Division Sales Manager.

Interviews for the post in question are being held in London at the Novotel at Heathrow Airport during the weekend of July 19–20. We are inviting suitable candidates to attend for a preliminary interview on the Saturday. On the Sunday short-listed candidates will then proceed to a second round of interviews conducted by a panel made up of our Human Resources Manager and staff.

All short-listed candidates will be notified approximately 10 days after interview.

Travel and accommodation expenses will be borne by the company for all candidates living outside the UK who are invited to interview.

Please confirm your participation by return, indicating your time of arrival.

Yours sincerely
AIR SPACE FREIGHT FORWARDING

Henry Fuller
Human Resources Division

European Division
  División Europea
preliminary
  preliminar
short-listed
  candidates
  candidatos
  seleccionados
proceed proceder
panel comisión
human resources
  recursos humanos
staff personal
notify notificar
participation
  participación
time of arrival
  hora de llegada

3rd April 20..

To whom it may concern

Ms MARÍA GAYTE SAMPEDRO

Ms Gayte worked with Technology Transfer Systems Ltd as Departmental Head in our software development and documentation department during the period from 1 January 20.. to 31 March 20..

After having rapidly taken stock of the resources available in this department, both in terms of manpower and technology, she was able to proceed to evaluating its strengths and weaknesses. Her restructuring of the section led to an immediate improvement in morale and performance resulting in greater efficiency and dedication from all concerned.

The areas for which she took responsibility involved many skills: documenting, typing and layout of a user manual, testing the software system during development and liaising with software engineers as bugs or queries were raised.

Her ability to chair meetings and conduct them in a manner conducive to constructive results has proved invaluable in the course of her three years with our company.

Technology Transfer Systems Ltd will sadly miss the skills and dedication of which Ms Gayte's departure will deprive the company. We do not hesitate to recommend her to any future employer.

Yours faithfully

...

to whom it may concern *aquí:* a quien pueda interesar
Departmental Head Jefe de Departamento
software development desarrollo de software
take stock hacer inventario
resource recurso, medio
manpower mano de obra
efficiency eficiencia, rendimiento
dedication dedicación
layout diseño, presentación
user manual manual del usuario
liaise enlazar/ actuar de enlace
bug error
chair presidir
conducive to propicio para

75 Rechazo de solicitud
Rejection of an application

September 15, 20..

Mr Daniel Rivas López
Rda. Guinardó, 91
08025 Barcelona
Spain

Dear Mr Rivas

Thank you for your letter of September 1, in which you apply for the post of European Sales Co-ordinator.

Having studied your résumé, references and testimonials we have come to the conclusion that your particular area of expertise lies in transport logistics and human resources management. What we are looking for, however, is a candidate who is an advertising and marketing specialist. For this reason we are unable to offer you the post in question.

As we feel that your skills could be used elsewhere in our European operation, we have passed your application on to our European Transport Dept., where it will be put on file pending a future vacancy.

With best wishes for the future,

Yours truly,
INTERNATIONAL ELECTRONICS INC

Benjamin Rhodes
Personnel Manager

European Sales Co-ordinator
Coordinador de Ventas en Europa
résumé
curriculum vitae
testimonial
recomendación/ referencia
transport logistics
logística de transportes
human resources management
dirección de recursos humanos
advertising specialist
especialista en publicidad
put on file
archivar
pending a future vacancy
en espera de una futura vacante
Personnel Manager
Director de Personal

3 February 20..

National Chiswick Bank Ltd
Chiswick High Road Branch
27 Chiswick High Road
Chiswick
London W4T 6PP
England

For the attention of the Manager

Dear Sir or Madam

As our company has enjoyed excellent relations with your bank in the past we would be most grateful if you could assist our newly appointed Market Research Co-ordinator (UK Division), Mr Juan Romero Julián, on his arrival in London at the beginning of next month.

He has been entrusted with the task of drawing up energy consumption profiles for major energy users in the process engineering sector in the south of England and would therefore appreciate any assistance your bank can give him as regards potential customers and their suitability. We feel that your wide experience in dealing with corporate customers and the considerable skill with which you have handled our affairs in the past will greatly aid Mr Romero in this undertaking.

We wish to take this opportunity to extend our thanks to you in advance for any assistance given to him in this matter and remain,

Yours faithfully
Energía Rovira, S.L.
...

excellent relation
  relación excelente
newly appointed
  nombrado recientemente
market research
  estudio de mercado
draw up   elaborar
energy consumption profile
  perfil del consumo energético
process engineering
  técnica/proceso de fabricacion
potential customer
  cliente potencial
suitability
  idoneidad
corporate customer
  cliente corporativo
undertaking
  tarea, labor
extend   *aquí:*
  expresar

Europlast Inc.
2009 Danbury Road
Wilton
Connecticut
USA

31 March 20..

New Channel Ltd
Unit 6
Hadrian Industrial Estate
Cambridge CA4 9UJ
England

Dear Mr Rogers

Our New Representive, Mr David Klein

We are pleased to inform you that, as from May 1st of this year, Mr David Klein will be our new representative in the south of England. He will be taking over from Mr Robert Smile, who will be returning to the USA for a post of responsibility in Connecticut.

Mr Klein will be moving to the UK after a highly successful spell in Canada where he represented our interests from January 20.. to March 20... In the course of his employment with our company, Mr Klein has been able to amass an enviable amount of knowledge as regards local market requirements and customers' expectations and his sound technical background has enabled him to diagnose customer needs quickly and accurately.

You may rest assured that the high standard of service you have come to expect from our company will remain available to all our customers and that all contracts, agreements and arrange-

...../2

spell *aquí:* estancia
represent interests
 representar intereses
employment
 empleo, trabajo
amass acumular
as regards con
 respecto a, relativo a
**local market
 requirements**
 necesidades del
 mercado local
**customers'
 expectations**
 expectativas
 del cliente
**technical
 background**
 formación técnica
customer needs
 necesidades
 del cliente
high standard
 alto nivel

ments between yourselves and our organisation will in no way be affected by the new appointment.

Mr Klein will be calling upon you in the near future to introduce himself personally and is looking forward to meeting our existing business partners and also expanding our operation in the UK.

Should you have any queries as regards future arrangements we will be pleased to provide you with any information you may require.

Yours sincerely
EUROPLAST Inc.

Peter Wood
Sales Co-ordinator

arrangement
convenio, acuerdo
appointment
nombramiento
call upon s.o.
visitar a alguien
introduce oneself
presentarse
uno mismo
operation *aquí:*
actividad, negocio

Transportes Martín
San Francisco, 41
33015 Oviedo
Spain

15 April 20..

Balcombes Insurance Loss Assessor,
Surveyors and Valuers
2 Paradise Row
London E2 4PB
England

Dear Sirs

Vehicle Damage and Part-Loss of Load

Please assess the costs arising from the damage to
our vehicle Reg. No. O-2434-MP and its load (motor
vehicle components) when it was involved in an
accident with an oncoming lorry on the approach
road to Dover Eastern Docks on April 12th.

The vehicle and the remaining part of the load were
recovered by:

Crowvale Haulage Ltd
(Commerical Vehicle Recovery Services)
Silverdale House
Pump Lane
London W5 7UJ

Tel. 0181 573 2624

at whose premises they can be examined during
usual working hours by appointment.

The Dover Constabulary has made a report on
the accident and an investigation into the collision

...../2

Surveyor *aquí:*
  inspector (técnico)
Valuer tasador
vehicle damage
  daño del vehículo
part-loss
  pérdida parcial
load carga
motor vehicle
  component
  pieza del automóvil
approach road
  calle de acceso
haulage transporte
  (por carretera)
commercial vehicle
  recovery service
  servicio de
  recuperación
  de vehículos
  comerciales
usual working
  hours
  horario laboral
by appointment
  con cita previa

is being conducted by Detective Constable Ralf Hayes.

We also enclose on a separate sheet from our insurers, Star Insurance, a list of points which should be considered in your report.

Please submit your report and invoice in triplicate to ourselves as soon as possible to enable us to make a claim to our insurers.

Yours faithfully
Transportes Martín

Julián Alcaraz Bella
Transport Manager

Enc

detective constable
agente de policía
invoice factura
in triplicate
por triplicado

Prendergast & Johnson
Investment Consultants
52 Carter Lane
London EC2 6ZG
England

FG/FB
10 February 20..

Robles Inversiones, S.A.
Avda. Alberto Alcocer, 19
28016 Madrid
Spain

Dear Mr Rodríguez

Current UK Stock Market Trends

Yesterday's sharp fall in the value of the pound
on the foreign exchange market led to alarm in
the City that inflation would increase again and
no further interest rate cuts would be forthcoming
from the Government.

The current decline in the value of the pound
against the dollar is increasing industry's raw
materials and fuel bill. Sterling is currently being
traded at $1.4155.

General apprehensiveness among dealers has
wiped almost £8 billion off share values with the
FT-SE-100 index closing 38.7 points lower at
2831.3. There has been a bout of profit-taking,
which served to depress share values still further
and it is rumoured that a number of debt-ridden
companies are intending to raise finance with
rights issues in the near future.

...../2

stock market trend
tendencia bursátil
**foreign exchange
market** mercado
de divisas
interest rate cut
recorte del tipo
de interés
be forthcoming
ser inminente
**raw materials and
fuel bill** materia
prima y coste
de la gasolina
wipe off borrar
share value valor
de las acciones
FT-SE índice
bursátil del
Financial Times
close ... points lower
cerrar con ... puntos
a la baja
bout *aquí:* racha
debt-ridden
endeudado
rights issue
emisión de derechos

A false rumour about the Kingfisher group's supposed intention to part-finance the takeover of the French electrical retailer Mercier with a rights issue made the group's shares lose 5p, ending the day down at 526p.

The banking sector was slightly depressed by the reversal of hopes on interest rate cuts. All the major banks lost between 9p–17p and there was also a significant volume of profit-taking.

In general, the market is turning defensive and this trend has been borne out by the latest figures from Dawson Europe, whose analysts have detected an underlying downturn in industrial output with only the water sector registering strong dividend growth.

Despite the current downward trend a monthly survey by Gallup of 101 institutions showed that 15% of them intended to increase their holdings of UK equities, up from 7% in January.

We feel it would be advisable to exercise caution for the next week or so until the rights issued have materialised and the Government has given a clear signal as regards its interest rate policy.

Should there be any last-minute developments we will fax you immediately.

Yours sincerely
PRENDERGAST & JOHNSON
...

p = points puntos
volume of profit-taking volumen de retirada de dividendos
bear out confirmar, demostrar
industrial output producción industrial
dividend growth crecimiento de dividendos
holdings participaciones
equities valores
interest rate policy política del tipo de interés

August 17, 20..

Hitech Software Inc.
400 Sunnyvale Boulevard
San José
California 94021
USA

Gentlemen:

Our Order of 1 August for 10 Site Licenses
for Software Application

We refer to our above-mentioned order for site
licenses for your Megamerge application and
wish to point out that, at the time of placing
our order, Megamerge 3.0 was the latest version
commercially available. As you have since brought
out Megamerge 3.1 we wish to amend our order
accordingly, as we only install state-of-the-art
software.

We trust this amendment will not bring about any
delay in delivery. Should this be the case please
fax us immediately.

Sincerely yours,
SORIA INFORMÁTICA

José Estrella Rivera
Proprietor

site license
  licencia de uso/
  instalación
**software
  application**
  aplicación
  de software
**at the time of
  placing our
  order**   en el
  momento de
  cursar nuestro
  pedido
**commercially
  available**
  comercialmente
  disponible
amend   modificar
state-of-the-art
  el más actualizado
bring about
  provocar, conllevar
Proprietor
  propietario

TVG/klt
19 July 20..

Europhar International Ltd
115 Gloucester Road
London W4 3HH
England

Attn: Mr William Mason, Export Sales Manager

Dear Mr Mason

Our Order No. 73F/03 Disposable Syringes
of 10 July 20..

With reference to the above-mentioned order we
wish to change the quantity required from 10,000
as originally stated to 15,000 disposable syringes.

We trust you will be able to accommodate us in
this matter and assume that the conditions agreed
still apply.

Please confirm this amendment in writing, stating
any change in delivery date. We are willing to
accept two part-deliveries (e.g. of 10,000 and
5,000 units) should this prove necessary.

Yours sincerely

Teresa Villalobos García
Purchasing Manager

disposable syringe
  jeringa desechable
as originally stated
  según lo establecido
  en un principio
accommodate
  satisfacer
apply *aquí:*
  estar en vigor
amendment
  modificación
delivery date
  fecha de entrega
part-delivery
  entrega parcial
unit unidad
**Purchasing
  Manager** Director
  de Compras

82

El proveedor no acepta el pedido
Supplier rejects order

12 August 20..

Riverside Organ Studios
50 Station Road
New Malden
Kent KT1 R55
England

Dear Mr Marshall

We confirm receipt of your order for two Vox Z1 47 synthesisers but regret having to inform you that Vox Ltd have now gone out of business – thus making it impossible for us to accept your order.

There is a wide variety of similar instruments on the UK market, however, and for your information we enclose our latest catalogue and price list.

At present orders for the instruments listed can be processed within 4 weeks of receipt of order.

Assuring you of our best attention at all times we remain,

Yours sincerely

Terry Webb
Export Sales

confirm receipt
acusar recibo, confirmar recepción
synthesiser
sintetizador
go out of business
cerrar el negocio
wide variety
amplia variedad
instrument
instrumento
process an order
llevar a cabo un pedido
within 4 weeks of receipt of order
en cuatro semanas a partir de la fecha de recepción del pedido

11 July 20..

PLANCO LTD
16 Garden Avenue
Harwich
Essex
CO12 4JR
Great Britain

Attn: Ms Anne Howard, Accounts

Dear Ms Howard

Your statement of account no. 5471 of 30 June 20..

Enclosed please find a copy of your statement up to and including 30th June 20.. showing a balance of £230.00 in your favour.

Unfortunately, we think there is a mistake in this statement. You have forgotten to credit us with £50.00, a reduction which you granted us on 5th May 20.. because one case of your delivery covering order no. 3099 arrived here in damaged condition.

Please check this statement again and if you agree with it we shall be pleased to receive your corrected version. We shall then remit the amount of £180.00 immediately to your account by banker's transfer.

Yours sincerely
Gutiérrez e Hijos, S.L.
...

statement of account extracto de cuenta
balance saldo
credit abonar
reduction reducción
grant conceder
covering que cubre
in damaged condition deteriorado, en malas condiciones
corrected version versión rectificada
remit transferir, depositar, ingresar
by banker's transfer por transferencia bancaria

13 Feb 20..

Thailand Timber Company
Wireless Road
Bangkok
Thailand

Dear Sir or Madam

We have received the B/L and insurance certificate for the consignment of 50 tons of palletised teak on board MV "August Moon", which is due to dock in Liverpool at the end of this month.

We note with dismay, however, that the Bs/L include the notation "6 pallets damaged". As you well know, our company sells timber "on water" to European importers and an unclean B/L is only negotiable in exceptional cases. We fail to understand why you did not provide the shipping company with a letter of indemnity as soon as it was apparent that the goods were not in perfect condition.

It only remains to be hoped that the damage is to the pallets and not to the timber. Should the consignment prove unsaleable we will review all future contracts with your company and seek redress for the loss of trade.

Yours faithfully
NORTHERN TIMBER LTD

J. B. Jones
Manager

B/L = bill of lading conocimiento de embarque
insurance certificate póliza de seguros
consignment partida
palletised teak madera de teca embalada en forma de *pallette*
MV = motor vessel buque, barco de motor
notation anotación
pallet *pallette*
unclean B/L conocimiento de con reservas/ embarque sucio
shipping company compañía naviera/ marítima
letter of indemnity carta de indemnización
unsaleable invendible
seek redress exigir compensación

25 February 20..

Sri Lanka Tea Traders
P.O. Box 1974
Colombo
Sri Lanka

Dear Mr Patel

We confirm receipt of the 30 chests of Ceylon
Pekoe tea ordered by ourselves on May 15th.

As agreed in the Contract of Sale we instructed
the Finchley Branch of the Benson Bank to arrange
for payment by Mail Payment Order through your
bank in Colombo. Instructions to this effect were
mailed to Sri Lanka today and we have been given
to understand that you will receive payment in
approximately a fortnight's time.

We look forward to doing further business with you
in the near future and remain,

Yours sincerely
FINCHLEY TRADING COMPANY

Daljit Singh
General Manager

chest   caja
contract of sale
   contrato de venta
instruct   dar
   instrucciones
branch   sucursal
arrange for
   payment
   disponer, ordenar
   el pago
instructions
   to this effect
   instrucciones
   al respecto
give to understand
   dar a entender

March 3rd, 20..

Messrs Miller & Smutts
95-101 East London Roads
Pietermaritzburg
South Africa

For the attention of Mr Ronald Miller

Dear Mr Miller

Advice of Draft re Your Order No. JK8/3/02 for
Agricultural Sprinklers

In accordance with the above-mentioned order the
3 irrigation systems ordered have been shipped on
board MV "Anastasia", CIF Durban. The vessel is
due to dock in Durban at the end of this month.

We enclose the following documents:

Commercial Invoice
Customs Invoice
Copy of B/L

The Durban branch of Benson International will
release the original Bs/L and the Insurance
Certificate upon acceptance of our draft drawn
upon yourselves at 30 d/s.

We trust the sprinklers will arrive punctually and in
good condition and look forward to the opportunity
of serving you in the future.

Yours sincerely
CARLOS SISTEMAS DE REGADÍO, S.L.
...

agricultural sprinkler aspersor agrícola
irrigation system sistema de regadío
CIF = cost, insurance, freight *(Incoterm)* costo, seguro y flete
commercial invoice factura comercial
customs invoice factura de aduanas
copy of B/L = bill of lading copia del conocimiento de embarque
insurance certificate póliza de seguros
draft letra, giro
at 30 d/s = days/sight a 30 días de vista

The Steel Box Company Ltd
Smithington Lane
Smithington
Sheffield SH7 4AG
England

TH/oq
27 February 20..

METALES RAMOS, S.L.
Gran Vía, 59
48001 Bilbao
Spain

Dear Sirs

<u>Outstanding Balances Due to your Company to Date</u>

We regret to inform you that the current worldwide recession in the steel industry has led to a collapse in the market for viably priced metal boxes made in Europe. The sad fact of the matter is that Eastern European and Far Eastern competitors have flooded our traditional sales territory with good-quality products at 75% of our rock-bottom prices.

We, ourselves, are unable to meet our financial obligations with respect to our bankers and suppliers, with the consequence that insolvency proceedings in accordance with the UK Insolvency Act of 1986 have been instituted against us by our first-ranking creditor, Benson Bank plc.

...../2

outstanding balance saldo pendiente
worldwide recession recesión mundial
steel industry industria del acero
viably priced metal boxes cajas metálicas a un precio viable
sales territory territorio de ventas
rock-bottom price precio más bajo posible
insolvency proceedings procedimiento de insolvencia
institute iniciar
first-ranking creditor acreedor más preferente

The liquidator appointed will wind up our company and pay preferential and secured creditors in full. Thereafter, non-prefential trading creditors such as yourselves with unsecured debts will be taken into consideration.

You will be informed in due course of the date of creditors' meeting, which all parties concerned will be invited to attend.

We hope you will appreciate that we are the victims of a situation entirely beyond our control and would stress the fact that we have been given assurances that the liquidator will treat all creditors equitably.

Yours faithfully
THE STEEL BOX COMPANY LTD

Terence Hill
Company Secretary

wind up   liquidar
preferential creditor   acreedor preferente
unsecured debts   deudas sin garantía de cobro
victim   víctima
beyond our control   ajeno a nuestro control
equitably   equitativamente

2 April 20..

Carpendale Wholesale Grocery Supplies Ltd
Unit 6
Highgate Trading Estate
London N8 9IP

Dear Sirs

We regret to inform you that the recent opening and proximity of a new branch of the "Cash & Carry Supergreen" greengrocer's chain has led to a disastrous decline in the trading situation of our business. This, in turn, has resulted in our no longer being able to meet our current and long-term financial obligations.

Our preferential creditors have obtained a receiving order, under the provisions of which we have been granted a month's grace, during which time we have the opportunity to reach an amicable settlement with our non-preferential creditors. Should we not achieve voluntary composition, the court will issue an adjudication order and appoint a trustee to take charge of liquidating our assets.

We would therefore respectfully invite you to attend the creditors' meeting which will take place on April 15 next on our premises.

You may rest assured that each application will be treated on its merits and in good faith.

Yours faithfully
QUICK TURNOVER GREENGROCERIES LTD

Harold Archer
Chief Accountant

wholesale
  mayorista
grocery supplies
  suministro de
  comestibles
trading estate
  inmueble comercial
trading situation
  situación comercial
preferential
  creditor   acreedor
  preferente
receiving order
  declaración de
  quiebra
provision
  condición
an amicable
  settlement
  acuerdo amigable
voluntary
  composition
  resolución de
  mutuo acuerdo
adjudication
  adjudicación
trustee
  administrador
  fideicomisario

89 Orden de compra de acciones
Order for shares

➡ carta 90

14 May 20..

SouthWestern Investment Centre
PO Box 205
Watford DW1 1BP
England

Portfolio No.: D/281248-2-03

Dear Sir or Madam

Please buy positions in the following shares in accordance with the limits indicated. A total value of £15,000 should not be exceeded.

a) TCC Shares   to the value of £5,000
b) EuroRoad Shares   to the value of £1,000
c) PowerGen   to the value of £9,000
(rights issue as per
allotment letter)
                       Total   £15,000

Please debit the appropriate amount to my South-Western Investor Account.

Yours faithfully

G. P. Courtney (Dr)

portfolio cartera
  de valores
share acción
total value
  valor total
exceed exceder
rights issue
  emisión de
  derechos
allotment letter
  notificación de
  reparto, carta
  de asignación
debit adeudar
appropriate
  amount
  cantidad asignada
investor account
  cuenta del inversor

Extracto de cuentas semestral
de la distribución de acciones
Half-yearly share dealing account statement

➡ carta 89

30 June 20..

Dr G. P. Courtney
Trantenrother Weg 56
58455 Witten
Germany

Portfolio No.: D/281248-2-03

Dear Dr Courtney

PORTFOLIO VALUATION STATEMENT

We are pleased to forward as per the enclosed
your Portfolio statement for the first half of 20..

The statement itemises your current investments,
their original cost and current market price, their
yield and the total value of your holdings. The
Contract Notes from share deals concluded in the
course of the last week are also enclosed.

All profits accruing have been credited to your
SouthWestern Investor Account, which currently
shows a net balance of £17,789.95 in your favour.

We look forward to serving you in the future and
remain,

Yours sincerely
SOUTHWESTERN INVESTMENT CENTRE

P. K. Hodgkith
Portfolio Manager

Encs

portfolio valuation
  tasación de la
  cartera de valores
itemise   detallar,
  especificar
current investment
  inversión actual
market price
  precio de mercado
yield   rendimiento
  financiero,
  beneficio
holdings
  aquí: posesión
contract note
  facturación
  de compra
share deal   negocio
  de acciones
accruing profit
  beneficio devengado
credit   abonar
net balance
  saldo neto
Portfolio Manager
  Gestor de la Cartera
  de Valores

Lowndes Lambert
Trading Group
Bullrush Lane
London E3 8JL

GL/bk
9 June 20..

Soler García
Arbitraje de mercancías
c/ San Andrés, 141
15003 La Coruña
Spain

Dear Sirs

We are currently involved in a dispute with the Tomás Internacional, S.L., La Coruña who have refused payment for a consignment of 4,000 sacks of robusta coffee from São Paulo in Brazil. The consignment is currently on board MV "Polixenes" in La Coruña.

They maintain, after having taken samples, that the quality of the coffee does not correspond to the description "best quality" as stated in the contract and have appointed an arbitrator to act on their behalf. The company representing their interests is Pedralbes, Arbitraje de mercancías, in La Coruña. A copy of their report is enclosed.

Our contract with Tomás Internacional provides for arbitrage in La Coruña and for our arbitrator to be notified of the name of Tomás Internacional's arbitrator within 7 days of appointment. In addition, all arbitrators are to be members of the Chamber of Commerce in the city in which the parties involved have registered their companies.

...../2

dispute conflicto
consignment partida
MV = motor vessel buque, barco de motor
take samples adquirir muestras
appoint nombrar
arbitrator árbitro
act on their behalf actuar en su nombre
provide for prever
within 7 days of appointment en siete días a partir del nombramiento
the parties involved las partes involucradas
register registrar

We would therefore be most grateful if you would act as our arbitrator in this matter. We are of the opinion that the quality of the consignment of coffee in question is well within the limits of the definition "best quality" and would request you to take samples from a large cross-section of the sacks making up the consignment.

We trust you will succeed in upholding our claim in this matter, thus obviating the need for an umpire to be appointed.

Yours faithfully
Lowndes Lambert Trading Group

Gerald Lambert
Director

Enc

be well within the limits cumplir con los requisitos
cross-section muestra representativa
make up *aquí:* componer, formar
uphold defender
obviate prevenir, evitar
umpire árbitro

Especificaciones del producto en un folleto
Product specifications in a brochure

23 August 20..

Dear Customer

Thank you for your enquiry regarding our products. We enclose a current brochure outlining our entire range and will be most pleased to assist you further with your choice of vehicle.

The content of the brochure enclosed is as accurate as possible from information available at the time of going to press. Dimensions, weights and plan drawings are approximate. Leisureworld Caravans (UK) Ltd reserves the right to alter specifications, colours, models and ranges as materials and conditions demand and, consequently, can accept no responsibility for discrepancies between information contained in this brochure and subsequent models. This brochure, therefore, does not constitute an offer by Leisureworld Caravans (UK) Ltd.

If, after having studied our sales literature, you require further information, please do not hesitate to contact one of our approved dealers in the UK, all of whose names, addresses, telephone and fax numbers are enclosed.

We look forward to the pleasure of serving you in the near future.

Yours faithfully
Leisureworld Caravans (UK) Ltd

Harvey Threadgold
General Manager

Encs

outline señalar, mostrar
range gama
choice elección
dimension medida
plan drawing planos
reserve the right reservar el derecho
alter alterar, modificar
consequently por consiguiente
accept responsibility aceptar la responsabilidad
discrepancy discrepancia
subsequent posterior
constitute constituir
sales literature folleto informativo
approved dealer concesionario oficial

Newtown Electronics
36 Barton Road
Hatfield
Herts HT9 7PQ

28 March 20..

Messrs Cotton, Gummersall & Palmer
Windsor House
1008 East End Road
London SW16 7UJ

Dear Sirs

Breach of Contract due to Delay in Delivery

We are writing to you to request you to represent our interests in what we consider to be a clear case of breach of contract.

From the correspondence enclosed you will note that "DV-Electronic Data Systems España, S.L." have failed to comply with the terms set out in our Contract of Sale (see enclosure), whereby delivery of the goods in question (viz 400 VGA Monitors, Type MultiSync XL) was assured by 15th January 20..

We finally took delivery of these articles on March 10th, by which time we had incurred considerable financial losses and were obliged to supply our customers at 25% under list price.
We have already deducted out losses from the invoice amount + 10% administration charges and transferred the amended invoice amount to DV-Electronic's account. We have, in addition, cancelled a further order (see enclosures) for 400 key-

.../2

breach of contract incumplimiento de contrato
delay in delivery demora en la entrega
data system sistema de datos
set out exponer
the goods in question la mercancía en cuestión
viz es decir
assure asegurar
be obliged verse obligado
at 25% under list-price un 25% menos de lo marcado en la lista de precios
deduct out deducir
invoice amount importe de la factura
administration charges gastos administrativos

boards. DV-Electronic, however, are insisting upon a list-price settlement and have indicated that they will not accept our cancellation. They have also passed the matter on to their solicitors, who have threatened litigation, should we fail to honour our order for the keyboards.

We welcome your comments on this matter and would be most grateful if you could act in such a manner as to convince DV-Electronic that any further attempt to press their claim would prove futile.

Yours faithfully
NEWTOWN ELECTRONICS

J. B. Butterson
Managing Director

Encs

pass the matter on to their solicitors
poner el asunto en manos de sus abogados

threaten litigation
amenazar con un litigio

honour an order
realizar un pedido, llevar a cabo un pedido

20 July 20..

Messrs Price Waterhouse
Management Consultants
Knightsbridge House
185 Knightsbridge
London SW7 90L

Dear Sirs

As a result of the lasting effects of the current recession, which has affected business badly in our field, we are now obliged to restructure our operation and will have no alternative but to retrench heavily.

We therefore require assistance with the shedding of workers by natural wastage or voluntary redundancy, severance pay, early retirement plans with or without a gratuity, redundancy schemes with retraining opportunities for younger workers and a public relations strategy to help make these inevitable measures more palatable to our employees and the public at large.

In addition, we will need to scrutinize our middle and upper management structures in order to weed out under-productive staff. Here, we will require assistance with assessment procedures to gauge performance and also with the implementation of decisions resulting from the discovery that particular individuals can no longer remain in our employ.

We would therefore request you to contact us immediately with a view to drawing up a profile of our company and putting forward short and medium-term strategies.

Yours faithfully
...

retrench reducir
shed workers reducir plantilla
natural wastage jubilaciones
voluntary redundancy despido voluntario
severance pay compensación por despido
early retirement plan plan de jubliación anticipada
gratuity gratificación
palatable agradable
scrutinize inspeccionar
weed out suprimir
under-productive staff personal poco productivo
assessment procedures procedimientos de evaluación
gauge performance valorar el rendimiento

Informe sobre un estudio de mercado
Market research report

June 25, 20..

Constance Cummings
Cosmetics Manufacturers
One World Trade Center
Suite 7691
New York, N.Y. 10048
USA

Gentlemen:

We are now in a position to provide you with the first results of our market survey on Spanish consumer habits as regards the use of cosmetics.

Our field-workers conducted a representative survey of females aged 15-60 years and completed a questionnaire with the test persons on their preferences as regards hair and skin preparations. Our survey incorporated questions on the recycling of packaging, vivisection issues and a possible multi-cultural image of society. In addition, we asked questions on matters such as manufacturing methods and the sourcing of ingredients used for beauty preparations (low-wage labor in the Third World, Amazon rain forest depletion, "natural" and "green" products, herbal remedies, cosmetic substances used by ancient cultures etc).

Our conclusions and recommendations are set out in detail in the charts included with this letter.

In essence, we recommend that the 15-25 year-old age group be approached with explicit reference to environmentally friendly products, developed on human test subjects and in no way involving the use of animals. Here a synthesis should be

...../2

market survey estudio de mercado
consumer habit hábitos del consumidor
questionnaire cuestionario
incorporate incluir
packaging embalaje
vivisection issue tema de vivisección
multi-cultural image of society imagen multi-cultural de la sociedad
manufacturing method método de fabricación
the Third World el Tercer Mundo
Amazon rain forest depletion deforestación de la selva tropical amazónica
herbal remedy remedio a base de hierbas

achieved between fashion-consciousness and "natural" beauty. We suggest using both European and African models in harmonious but also dynamic and exciting situations in your advertising.

The 25-40 year-olds will probably best respond to an "enlightened" and realistic approach to the problems of "getting the best out of your looks" with a little help from cosmetics. Here, an "intimate" approach is important, i.e. the cosmetic industry is secretly helping you to enhance your looks, whilst unsuspecting males think it's natural (hair rinses, skin toners, anti-wrinkle preparations).

The 45-60 year-olds will probably best respond to even more subtle allusions to the need for nature to be helped along a little, but here we recommend the idea of, "Go on, enjoy yourself now," or, "Treat yourself to something really good!" Prices for this age group can be increased by 5%-10% to underline market segmentation.

We trust you will be able to incorporate our suggestions in your advertising campaign and will be pleased to clarify any of our findings, should you request us to do so.

Sincerely yours,
DAWSON & DAWSON

A. Ruiz García
Senior Consultant

Encs

fashion-consciousness conciencia de moda
enhance resaltar
hair rinse tinte de cabello
skin toner tónico para la piel
anti-wrinkle preparation preparados antiarrugas
allusion alusión

➡ carta 97

HARVARD PLASTICS INC.
Broadway
New York, N.Y. 10018
USA

August 10, 20..

Human Resources Department
Harvard Plastics Inc. (UK)
Bull Ring Industrial Estate
Birmingham BI8 9LL
United Kingdom

Gentlemen:

European Languages Drive

As President of Harvard Plastics Inc. I take great
pleasure in utilizing this opportunity to address all
operatives in the Human Resources Departments
of our European subsidiaries. As you all know, we
are planning a considerable extension of our sales
territory, especially in Eastern Europe.

To this end I am issuing a Management Directive
to all Human Resources Departments to launch an
all-out effort to attract multilingual personnel at all
levels. The logistics at local level are entirely the
province of individual Human Resources Managers,
but let me make myself clear on this, we need
and expect results and an up-to-date profile of
all subsidiaries will be drawn up exactly one year
from now.

drive campaña
operative
  operativo
**Human Resources
  Department**
  Departamento de
  Recursos Humanos
**Management
  Directive**
  directiva para
  dirección
an all-out effort
  esfuerzo general
**multilingual
  personnel**
  personal plurilingüe
an up-to-date profile
  perfil actualizado

.../2

142

Existing employees must be encouraged to develop their language skills in their free time in courses run on company premises. Promotion prospects will be made dependent on this. Harvard Plastics are willing to refund employees' outlay on language tuition upon successful completion of a recognised qualification. Extra bonuses will be paid if an employee learns more than one foreign language. Furthermore, additional financial incentives will be made available to promote the study of Eastern European Languages such as Russian, Polish and Hungarian, for I feel that a sales thrust eastwards can only succeed if our personnel can operate through the medium of the language in the sales territory targeted.

I trust that our European Languages Drive Project will be crowned with success and feel sure a high degree of response throughout our organization will serve to secure jobs in the future.

Very truly yours,

Clarence C. Pollock
PRESIDENT

language skill
habilidad para
los idiomas
free time
tiempo libre
company premises
oficinas de
la empresa
promotion prospects
perspectivas
de promoción
employees' outlay
gastos de los
empleados
language tuition
clases de idiomas
**recognised
qualification**
título reconocido
sales thrust
impulso en
las ventas
sales territory
territorio de ventas

143

Respuesta al informe anual de la empresa matriz
Response to parent company's annual report

➜ carta 96

Harvard Plastics Inc. (UK)
Bull Ring Industrial Estate
Birmingham BI8 9LL
United Kingdom

4th July 20..

The President
Harvard Plastics Inc.
Broadway
New York, N.Y. 10018
USA

Dear Mr Pollock

We have studied your Annual Report for 20.. and come to the conclusion that the loss in pre-tax profits of $1.2bn incurred by Harvard Plastics worldwide was mainly attributable to high labour costs and import duty on plastics entering Europe.

The conclusion we have come to is that relocation of part of your manufacturing facilities in one of the cheaper EU countries (UK, Ireland, Portugal, Greece) may be the answer to import duties, for in this way the "80% local content" ruling as regards goods manufactured by companies in non-EU ownership can be complied with. Over 1,000 Japanese companies already have a production site in the UK alone.

We feel that every effort should be made to contact the municipalities in areas designated by the EU as "regional development areas" in order to obtain EU funding and low-priced land. We are convinced that any effort to bring jobs to Europe will be warmly welcomed by the government and local population

.../2

annual report
  informe anual
loss in pre-tax
  profits pérdida
  en las ganancias
  sin haber aplicado
  los impuestos
bn = billion
  mil millones
incur sufrir
relocation
  desplazamiento
manufacturing
  facilities
  instalaciones
  de fabricación
the 80% local
  content ruling
  regulación del 80%
  de la producción
  local
municipality
  municipio
designate designar
regional develop-
  ment area
  área de desarrollo
  regional
funding
  financiación

concerned, with good chances of highly favourable tax relief arrangements for an initial period and, especially in the UK, a pool of skilled labour available immediately.

Our Public Relations Department has already started to sound out local authorities in suitable areas in the UK and we will be sending you a report of our findings in good time for your AGM on 1 September.

You may rest assured that our recommendations will remain confidential, until such time as the matter of relocation in Europe has been discussed at the highest level.

Yours sincerely

Henry Wilberforce
Chief Executive
Harvard Plastics (UK)

tax relief
  desgravación fiscal
skilled labour
  mano de obra
  especializada
sound out
  hacer sondeos
**AGM = Annual
  General Meeting**
  asamblea/junta
  anual
confidential
  confidencial

➡ carta 99

Mediquip
Richmond Industrial Estate
Richmond
Surrey SU9 1JK
United Kingdom

12 July 20..

Núñez Médica, S.L.
c/ Orense, 105
28020 Madrid
Spain

Dear Sirs

<u>Medical and Surgical Instruments</u>

We are pleased to announce that our newly formed company "Mediquip Ltd", Company Registration No. 2391824, will start trading in Europe as from September 1st.

We specialise in the manufacture and distribution of high-quality medical apparatus and surgical equipment. In addition, we pioneer innovative ideas by inviting selected customers to test new apparatus made available to them at a fraction of cost price, thus making new techniques and treatments available to patients at affordable prices.

Our latest invention is a device for kidney operations without major surgery. Besides this we are currently promoting a local anaesthetic package to cut down the risks associated with surgery normally performed under general anaesthetic.

We include our catalogue and export price list for your information. All prices are quoted FOB UK airport.

...../2

manufacture fabricación
selected customers clientes seleccionados
make available poner a disposición
at a fraction of cost price a un precio muy inferior al de coste
at affordable prices a precios asequibles
device aparato, dispositivo
kidney operations operaciones de riñón
promote promocionar, promover
anaesthetic package equipo de anestesia
cut down reducir
perform surgery intervenir quirúrgicamente

Should you wish to be considered to take part in the testing of new devices please return the enclosed registration form. We would instal such devices at our own cost and offer attractive discounts on other orders to those participating.

We hope that we shall soon be able to supply you with your medical equipment needs. If you have any questions please do not hesitate to get in touch with us.

Yours faithfully
MEDIQUIP LTD

David Vance
Managing Director

Encs

medical equipment needs necesidades de equipos médicos

99

Contraoferta
Counter-offer

➡ carta 98

15 December 20..

Mediquip Ltd
Richmond Industrial Estate
Richmond
Surrey SU9 1JK
ENGLAND

Dear Sirs

Your Offer No. 1093 for Surgical Instruments

Thank you for the above-mentioned offer of
December 1st.

We have studied your prices and compared them
with those of your competitors and, despite being
well pleased with the quality of the goods, must
point out that your prices are some 10% too high
for the market here.

If you can see your way clear to accommodating
us with a 10% reduction we will be pleased to
place an order for the equipment listed on the
order form enclosed.

We look forward to your response to our proposal.

Yours faithfully
CLÍNICA DR. LIZANO

Antonio Rodríguez Fernández
Manager

**surgical
  instruments**
  instrumentos
  quirúrgicos
compare comparar
competitor
  competidor
be well pleased
  estar complacido
**if you can see your
  way clear**
  si existe alguna
  posibilidad
accommodate s.o.
  satisfacer, facilitar
order form
  hoja de pedido
proposal
  propuesta

17 August 20..

Enrique Gomírez Herrera
c/ Ponzano, 37
28010 Madrid
Spain

Dear Mr Enrique Gomírez

Many thanks for your valued enquiry as regards our range of cabin cruisers.

I have mailed you our brochure today by separate post and I trust it will be of interest. The price list is effective from 1st September 20.. and is for UK specifications.

I have asked our importer, "Moreno Importaciones, S.L.", Avda. Alberto Alcocer, 10, 28016 Madrid, Spain to confirm Spanish prices, Spanish speci-fications and also give you more detail about the products and built quality and other information you require.

In the meantime, if I can be of further assistance please contact me.

Yours sincerely
Mannepower International Ltd

Terence Perkins
Sales & Marketing Manager

cc Alfred Prentice

your valued enquiry
valiosa solicitud
as regards
referente
cabin cruiser
yate
by separate post
por correo aparte
be effective
entrar en vigor
specifications
aquí: normas
give more detail
facilitar más detalles
built quality
calidad de construcción/ fabricación

Apéndices

Moneda oficial de los países de habla inglesa

País	Moneda		Abreviatura	Subdivisión
	español	*inglés*		*inglés*
Australia	dólar australiano	Australian dollar	A$	100 cents
Bahamas	dólar bahamés	Bahamian dollar	B$	100 cents
Barbados	dólar de Barbados	Barbados dollar	BD$	100 cents
Canadá	dólar canadiense	Canadian dollar	C$	100 cents
Dominica	dólar del Caribe	East Caribbean dollar	EC$	100 cents
Estados Unidos de América	dólar estadounidense	United States dollar	(US) $	100 cents
Fidji	dólar de Fidji	Fiji dollar	F$	100 cents
Gran Bretaña e Irlanda del Norte	libra (esterlina)	pound (sterling)	£ (stg)	100 pence
Guyana	dólar de Guyana	Guyana dollar	G$	100 cents
Hong Kong	dólar de Hong Kong	Hong Kong dollar	HK$	100 cents
India	rupia india	Indian rupee	Rs	100 paise
Irlanda	euro	euro	€	100 cents
Jamaica	dólar jamaicano	Jamaican dollar	J$	100 cents
Liberia	dólar liberiano	Liberian dollar	L$	100 cents
Malasia	ringgit	ringgit	M$	100 sen
Malawi	kwacha de Malawi	Malawi kwacha	MK	100 tambala
Malta	lira maltesa	lira, *pl.* liri	LM	100 cents
Mauricio	rupia de Mauricio	Mauritius rupee	MauR	100 cents
Nigeria	naira	naira	N	100 kobo
Nueva Zelanda	dólar neozelandés	New Zealand dollar	NZ$	100 cents
Seychelles	rupia de Seychelles	Seychelles rupee	SR	100 cents
Singapur	dólar de Singapur	Singapore dollar	S$	100 cents
Sudáfrica	rand	rand	R	100 cents
Tanzania	chelín tanzano	Tanzanian shilling	TSh	100 cents
Uganda	chelín ugandés	Uganda shilling	USh	100 cents
Zambia	kwacha de Zambia	Zambian kwacha	K	100 ngwee
Zimbabwe	dólar zimbabwés	Zimbabwe dollar	Z$	100 cents

Medidas y pesos británicos y estadounidenses

Medidas de longitud

1 inch	= 2,54 cm	
1 foot	= 12 inches	= 30,48 cm
1 yard	= 3 feet	= 91,44 cm
1 (statute) mile		
	= 1760 yards	= 1,609 km

Medidas náuticas

1 fathom	= 6 feet	= 1,829 m
1 nautical mile		
	= 1,852 km	

Medidas de capacidad (GB)

Medidas para áridos y líquidos

1 gill	= 0,142 l	
1 pint	= 4 gills	= 0,568 l
1 quart	= 2 pints	= 1,136 l
1 gallon	= 4 quarts	= 4,5459 l
1 quarter	= 64 gallons	= 290,935 l

Medidas para áridos

1 peck	= 2 gallons	= 9,092 l
1 bushel	= 4 pecks	= 36,368 l

Medidas para líquidos

1 barrel	= 36 gallons	= 163,656 l

Medidas de capacidad (EE UU)

Medidas para áridos

1 pint	= 0,5506 l	
1 quart	= 2 pints	= 1,1012 l
1 gallon	= 4 quarts	= 4,405 l
1 peck	= 2 gallons	= 8,8096 l
1 bushel	= 4 pecks	= 35,2383 l

Medidas para líquidos

1 gill	= 0,1183 l	
1 pint	= 4 gills	= 0,4732 l
1 quart	= 2 pints	= 0,9464 l
1 gallon	= 4 quarts	= 3,7853 l
1 barrel	= 31.5 gallons	
	= 119,228 l	
1 barrel petroleum		
	= 42 gallons	= 158,97 l

Medidas de superficie

1 square inch	= 6,452 cm^2	
1 square foot	= 144 square inches	
	= 929,029 cm^2	
1 square yard	= 9 square feet	
	= 8361,26 cm^2	
1 acre	= 4840 square yards	
	= 4046,8 m^2	
1 square mile	= 640 acres	
	= 259 ha	
	= 2,59 km^2	

Medidas de peso

1 grain	= 0,0648 g	
1 dram	= 27.3438 grains	
	= 1,772 g	
1 ounce	= 16 drams	= 28,35 g
1 pound	= 16 ounces	= 453,59 g
1 hundredweight		
	= 1 quintal	
GB	= 112 pounds	
	= 50,802 kg	
EE UU	= 100 pounds	
	= 45,359 kg	
1 (long) ton		
GB	= 20 hundredweights	
	= 1016,05 kg	
1 (short) ton		
EE UU	= 20 hundredweights	
	= 907,185 kg	
1 stone	= 14 pounds	= 6,35 kg
1 quarter		
GB	= 28 pounds	
	= 12,701 kg	
EE UU	= 25 pounds	
	= 11,339 kg	

Medidas de volumen

1 cubic inch	= 16,387 cm^3	
1 cubic foot	= 1728 cubic inches	
	= 0,02832 m^3	
1 cubic yard	= 27 cubic feet	
	= 0,7646 m^3	

Nota: en inglés, los decimales van separados por un punto.

Abreviaturas comerciales

a.a.r.	against all risks	a todo riesgo
a/c	account	cuenta corriente
a/d	after date	posdatado, después de la fecha
AF	advance freight	anticipo sobre el flete
AGM	annual general meeting	junta general anual
a.m.	ante meridiem	antes del mediodía
amt.	amount	importe
approx.	approximately	aproximadamente
art.	article	artículo
A/S	account sales	cuenta de ventas
ASAP	as soon as possible	lo antes posible
ATM	automated teller machine	cajero automático
Bdy.	broadway	tipo de vía pública en EE UU y GB
B/E (B(s)/E)	bill(s) of exchange	letra(s) de cambio
B/L (B(s)/L)	bill(s) of lading	conocimiento(s) de embarque
bn	billion	mil millones
Bros.	brothers	hermanos
c./ca.	circa	alrededor de
CAD	cash against documents	pago contra documentos
cc	carbon copy	copia mecanográfica
C.C.	charges collect	portes debidos
CFR	cost and freight	costo y flete
CIF	cost insurance freight	costo, seguro y flete
CIP	carriage and insurance paid to	transportes y seguro pagados
c/o	care of	cuidado de
Co	company	compañía
COD	cash on delivery	entrega contra reembolso
COS	cash on shipment	embarque contra reembolso
c.p.d.	charterer pays dues	derechos pagados por el fletador
CPT	carriage paid to	portes pagados
cr.	creditor/credit	acreedor/crédito
c.r.	current rates	tipo de cambio actual
Cres.	crescent	tipo de vía pública en GB
c.t.	conference terms	condiciones de la conferencia
cv	curriculum vitae	currículum vitae
cwt.	hundredweight	50,802 kg en GB, 45,359 kg en EE UU
D/A	deposit account	cuenta de ahorros
D/A	documents against acceptance	aceptación contra documentos
DAF	delivered at frontier	entregado en frontera
d/d	days after date	días transcurridos desde el vencimiento

155

DDP	delivered duty paid	mercancía entregada con los derechos pagados
DDU	delivered duty unpaid	mercancía entregada con los derechos no pagados
def.	deferred	diferido, aplazado
dep.	departure	salida
DEQ	delivered ex quay	mercancía entregada en muelle
DES	delivered ex ship	mercancía entregada en buque
div.	dividend	dividendo
doz.	dozen	docena
D/P	documents against payment	pago contra documentos
Dr	Doctor	Doctor
d/s	days after sight	días vista (d/v)
E.& O.E.	errors and omissions excepted	salvo error u omisión
EEA	Exchange Equalisation Account	cuenta de compensación de cambios
EFTPOS	Electronic funds transfer at the point of sale	transferencia electrónica de fondos en punto de venta
e.g.	exempli gratia, for example	por ejemplo (por ej.)
EMS	European Monetary System	Sistema Monetario Europeo
EMU	European Monetary Union	Unión Monetaria Europea
encl, enc(s)	enclosure(s)	anexo(s)
E.O.M.	end of month	fin de mes
ERM	Exchange Rate Mechanism	mecanismo de cambio de divisas
ETA	estimated time of arrival	hora prevista de llegada
etc	et cetera, and so on	etcétera (etc.)
e.t.c.	expected to complete	listo para desembarcar
e.t.s.	expect to sail	listo para zarpar
EXW	ex works	en fábrica, franco fábrica
f.a.q.	fair average quality	calidad normal
FAS	free alongside ship	franco al costado del buque
fc.	for cash	al contado
FCA	free carrier	franco transportista
FCR	forwarding agent's certificate of receipt	certificado de recepción de la mercancía (hecho por el transportista)
FCT	forwarding agent's certificate of transport	certificado de transportes del transportista
FIFO	first in first out	primero en entrar, primero en salir
FOB	free on board	franco a bordo
FOR	free on rail	franco en ferrocarril
FPA	free from particular average	libre de avería particular
ft. (')	foot, feet	pie, pies
FTSE	Financial Times Stock Exchange Index	índice bursátil del *Financial Times*

GA	General Agent	Representante General (RG)
Gds.	gardens	tipo de vía pública en GB
HGV	heavy goods vehicle	vehículo de carga pesada
HMS	Her (His) Majesty's Ship (Steamer)	embarcación de la monarquía británica
H.P.	horse power	caballo de vapor (CV)
HP	hire purchase	compra a plazos
ICC	institute cargo clauses	cláusulas de flete del instituto
i.e.	id est, that is to say	id est, es decir
IMO	International Money Order	orden de pago internacional
in. (")	inch	pulgada
Inc.	incorporated with limited liability (EE UU)	sociedad anónima (S.A.) en EE UU
incl.	including	incluyendo
INCOTERMS	International Commercial Terms	términos de comercio internacional
IOU	"I owe you"	pagaré, abonaré
JV	joint venture	empresa conjunta
K	thousand	mil
kg	kilogram	kilogramo (kg)
lb (lbs)	pound(s)	libra(s)
L/C (L(S)/C)	letter(s) of credit	carta(s) de crédito
LIFO	last in first out	último en entrar, primero en salir
l/s	lump sum	suma global
Ltd	limited	sociedad anónima (S.A.) en GB
m	million	millón
m/a	my account	mi cuenta
m/d	months after date	meses transcurridos desde el vencimiento
mdse.	merchandise	mercancía
Messrs	Messieurs	Señores (Sres.)
MLR	minimum lending rate	tasa de préstamo mínimo
M.O.	money order	orden de pago
Mr	Mister	Señor
M/R	mate's receipt	albarán de embarque
Mrs		Señora de
Ms		Señora de, Señorita
m/s	months after sight	meses vencidos
MS	motor ship	buque, barco de motor
MV	motor vessel	buque, barco de motor
N/A	not applicable	no aplicable
nd (2nd)	second	segundo(a) (2°, 2ª)
No(s)	number(s)	número(s) (núm.)
NSF	no sufficient funds	fondos insuficientes
Nt	net terms	condiciones netas
O/o	to the order of	a la orden de

oz(s)	ounce(s)	onza(s)
p.a.	per annum	por año
pc(s)	piece(s)	pieza(s)
pd	paid	pagado
PIN	personal identity number	número de identificación personal
plc	public limited company	sociedad pública de responsabilidad limitada en GB
p.m.	post meridiem	después del mediodía
P.O. Box	Post Office Box	apartado/casilla de correos
P.O.	postal order	giro postal
p.o.d.	paid on delivery	pago a la entrega
pp	per pro(curationem)	por poder, en nombre de (p.p.)
ppd	pre-paid	pagado por adelantado
P.S.	postcript	posdata (P.D.)
p.t.o.	please turn over	ver al dorso, sigue al dorso
Pty	proprietary company, a private limited company registered in South Africa or Australia	sociedad privada de responsabilidad limitada, en Sudáfrica o Australia
q.v.	quod vide	que ve
rd (3rd)	third	tercero(a) (3º, 3ª)
recd.	received	recibido
regd.	registered	registrado
R.O.G.	receipt of goods	recepción de la mercancía
R.P.	reply paid	respuesta pagada
rsvp	répondez s'il vous plaît	se ruega contestación (s.r.c.)
S/A	Statement of Account	extracto de cuenta
sgd.	signed	firmado
Sqr.	square	plaza
SR&CC	(free from) strikes, riots and civil commotion	(libre de) huelgas, tumultos y desórdenes públicos
S.S.	steamship	buque, barco (de vapor)
st (1st)	first	primero(a) (1º, 1ª)
th (4th, 5th...)	fourth, fifth...	cuarto(a), quinto(a) (4º, 4ª), (5º, 5ª)...
Through B/L, Thru B/L	through bill of lading	a través de un conocimiento de embarque
T.T.	telegraphic transfer	transferencia telegráfica
v.	vide	véase
VAT	value added tax	impuesto sobre el valor añadido (IVA)
viz	videlicet	a saber, es decir
W(P)A	with (particular) average	con avería (particular)
WB, w/b	waybill (EE UU)	carta de porte
wt.	weight	peso
yd.	yard	yarda

Organizaciones internacionales

APEC	Asia Pacific Economic Cooperation	Cooperación Económica de Asia y el Pacífico (CEAP)
BSI	British Standards Institution	asociación británica de normalización
BT	British Telecom	compañía británica de telecomunicaciones
CBI	Confederation of British Industry	confederación británica de organizaciones empresariales
CEN	European Committee for Standardization	Comité Europeo de Normalización (CEN)
ECB	European Central Bank	Banco Central Europeo (BCE)
EFTA	European Free Trade Association	Asociación Europea de Libre Comercio (AELC)
EIB	European Investment Bank	Banco Europeo de Inversiones (BEI)
ERP	European Recovery Programme	Programa de Recuperación Europea
ETUC	European Trade Union Confederation	Confederación Europea de Sindicatos (CES)
EU	European Union	Unión Europea
GATT	General Agreement on Tariffs and Trade	Acuerdo General de Aranceles y Comercio
GPO	General Post Office	Correos británicos
IATA	International Air Transport Association	Asociación Internacional de Transporte Aéreo (IATA)
IBCC	International Bureau of Chambers of Commerce	Oficina Internacional de Cámaras de Comercio
IBRD	International Bank for Reconstruction and Development	Banco Internacional para la Reconstrucción y el Desarrollo (BIRD)
ICAO	International Civil Aviation Organisation	Organización de Aviación Civil Internacional
ICC	International Chamber of Commerce	Cámara de Comercio Internacional (CCI)
IDB	Inter-American Development Bank	Banco Interamericano de Desarrollo (BID)
IEA	International Energy Agency	Agencia Internacional de la Energía (AIE)

IMF	International Monetary Fund	Fondo Monetario Internacional (FMI)
ISO	International Standards Organisation	Organización Internacional de Normalización (OIN)
MOT (test)	Ministry of Transport (Test)	Inspección Técnica de Vehículos (ITV)
NAFTA	North American Free Trade Agreement	Tratado de Libre Comercio del Atlántico Norte (TLC)
NATO	North Atlantic Treaty Organisation	Organización del Tratado de Atlántico Norte (OTAN)
NCM-UK	NCM Credit Insurance Limited	Sucesor de la compañía de seguros *ECGD (Export Credit Guarantee Department)* del gobierno británico. Corresponde a la CESCE (Compañía Española de Seguros de Créditos de la Exportación)
OECD	Organisation for Economic Co-operation and Development	Organización para la Cooperación y el Desarrollo Económico (OCDE)
OPEC	Organisation of Petroleum Exporting Countries	Organización de los Países Exportadores de Petróleo (OPEP)
SITPRO	Simplification of International Trade Procedures Board	Comisión para la Simplificación del Comercio Internacional
SWIFT	Society for Worldwide Interbank Financial Telecommunication	Sociedad para las Telecomunicaciones Financieras Interbancarias Internacionales (SITF)
TUC	Trades Union Congress	confederación de los sindicatos británicos
UNCED	United Nations Conference on Environment and Development	Conferencia de las Naciones Unidas sobre Medio Ambiente y Desarrollo
UNCTAD	United Nations Conference on Trade and Development	Conferencia de las Naciones Unidas sobre Comercio y Desarrollo
UNIDO	United Nations Industrial Development Organisation	Organización de las Naciones Unidas para el Desarrollo Industrial (ONUDI)
WTO	World Trade Organisation	Organización Mundial de Comercio (OMC)

Diseños de cartas y sobres

1. Texto justificado

 LANCASHIRE
ENTERPRISES plc

Enterprise House
17 Ribblesdale Place · Winckley Square
Preston PR1 3NA
Tel: (01772) 203020 · Fax (01772) 204129
Telex: 67257 LANENT G

Your ref.:   EP/lf
Our ref.:   PA/ml

14 March 2000

Mr Enrique Prada Riera
Europlástico, S.L.
De la Bolsa, 7
28013 Madrid
Spain

Dear Mr Prada

Your enquiry of 2 March 2000

Thank you very much for your recent enquiry about our products and those of the firms we represent. We enclose our current catalogue and price lists, together with our terms of delivery. Discounts are, of course, dependent on the size of the order submitted.

We would be only too happy to send you samples of specific products, subject to certain conditions, or to arrange for a representative to visit you and help you to define your needs more closely. If you have any questions, please do not hesitate to contact me or our Sales Manager, Annette Mason, at the telephone number above. We look forward to hearing from you shortly.

Yours sincerely
Lancashire Enterprises plc

J. L. Palmerstone

J. L. Palmerstone
Managing Director

Enc

cc: Annette Mason, Sales Dept.

Lancashire House
Watery Lane
Preston PR2 2XE
Tel.: (01772) 203020
Fax (01772) 721029

Registered office:
Enterprise House · 17 Ribblesdale Place
Winckley Square · Preston PR1 3NA
Registered in England and Wales No: 2401383
A member of IMRO

Lancaster House
36 rue Breydel
1040 Brussels
Belgium
Tel: 32 2 230 34 38

2. Carta estadounidense justificada con puntuación en el saludo y en la despedida

---

The InterStay Hotel

1114 Seventh Avenue
New York, NY 10033
phone 212 383 4621
fax   212 383 4678

April 20, 2000

Mr. Alfredo Montes Rosal
Sánchez Import Export, S.L.
Calle 13, nº 160
Bogotá 1, D.E.
Colombia

Dear Mr. Montes:

This letter confirms your reservation for a double room with bath for July 16–20.

We have also reserved our conference facilities in the Manhattan Suite for your exclusive use on July 19 until 11 p.m. The room seats up to 15 people comfortably and will satisfy your needs for a small, but intensive one-day conference. We enclose our information material which, we hope, will answer your remaining questions.

Please let us know your further requirements, for example, as regards support facilities (video, tape recorders, etc) as soon as possible. May we also ask you to request your conference guests who would like to book their own rooms in the hotel to contact us at an early date.

Sincerely yours,

The InterStay Hotel

Samuel B. Long
General Manager

Enclosures

162

3. Sangría de la primera línea y puntuación en el saludo y en la despedida

Southall Groceries

42 Clarence Parade
Southall
Middlessex
MX3 6ZZ
Tel. (0181) 249 5462

14th February, 2000

The Hackney Trading Company Ltd,
120 –124 Canal Road,
LONDON NW3 6GH

Dear Sirs,

Thank you for your letter of February 1st in which you inform us that your company is to cease trading due to the early retirement of Mr Newbury. We were saddened by the news as you have been a reliable trading partner over the last few years. May we take this opportunity of wishing Mr Newbury all the very best for his retirement.

We shall be placing a further large order with you before the deadline for orders expires on March 31st. We should be grateful, however, if you could recommend in due course a firm which can supply us to your own high standards after this date.

Yours faithfully,

Terence Jones

Terence Jones
Proprietor

4. Sobre con dirección (Gran Bretaña)

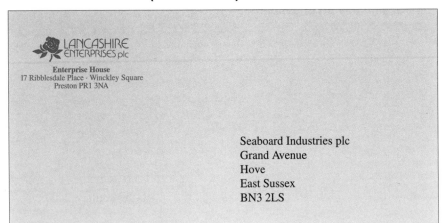

Enterprise House
17 Ribblesdale Place · Winckley Square
Preston PR1 3NA

Seaboard Industries plc
Grand Avenue
Hove
East Sussex
BN3 2LS

5. Sobre con dirección (Estados Unidos)

The InterStay Hotel

1114 Seventh Avenue
New York, NY 10033

MR JOHN D ENRIGHT
COMPUTRONIC INC
PO BOX 8732
AUSTIN TX 75110

Índice alfabético y temático

Las cifras remiten al número de las cartas-tipo.